PRAISE

"Every author should read this before buying or creating a book cover. It's an A-to-Z instruction manual for how to get a fantastic cover that sells books, and it's filled to the brim with practical advice. DO NOT miss out on the side-by-side examples of bad and good designs—your eyes will get an education."
JOHN FOX, OWNER OF BOOKFOX

"Jessica Bell pulls no punches as she shares her wealth of experience with you. This is a book full to the brim with actionable, clear advice. Learn why covers matter, the secrets of colors and layouts, how to pick designers and work with them, what horrors and pitfalls to avoid. Bonus: I've never read a guidebook that made me laugh as often as this one did! Jessica's honesty, directness and wit make *Can You Make the Title Bigga?* an utter joy to read."
LORNA FERGUSSON, AUTHOR, EDITOR, WRITING COACH

"A must-read for authors and cover designers that will save time and avoid disappointment! The appendix of questionnaires and contracts clarifies all you need to know to stay clear of the terrible misunderstandings that can happen between author and cover designer, and the humorous anecdotes show why such misunderstandings happen. Although I laughed at the authors' replies to designer questions, I blushed too—guilty as charged, on some counts. If you start reading this, you won't stop—and you will get something to take away, however much you know about book cover design."
JEAN GILL, AWARD-WINNING AUTHOR

"Essential and easy reading for anyone who wants to understand the subtle art of what makes a great book cover."
DEBBIE YOUNG, AUTHOR AND PUBLISHING COACH

"Everything you need to know—along with everything you didn't know you needed—in one entertaining and thorough book on cover design. This goes well beyond a dry textbook on the subject and really explains book cover design in the most clear, comprehensive way I've ever seen. And you'll get a laugh out of some of the author mishaps and the distinct voice of the author."
AMIE MCCRACKEN, AUTHOR, EDITOR, BOOK DESIGNER

can You make the Title the Bigga?

The Chemistry of Book Cover Design

jess!ca Bell

Can You Make the Title Bigga?
The Chemistry of Book Cover Design
Copyright © 2022 Jessica Bell
All rights reserved.

Print Edition
ISBN: 978-618-86077-6-7
Published by Vine Leaves Press in Greece 2022

No parts of this publication may be reproduced, stored in a retrieval system, or transmitted in any form or by any means, electronic, mechanical, photocopying, recording, or otherwise, without the prior written permission of the copyright owner.

This book is sold subject to the condition that it shall not, by way of trade or otherwise, be lent, resold, hired out, or otherwise circulated without the publisher's prior consent in any form of binding or cover other than that in which it is published and without a similar condition including this condition being imposed on the subsequent purchaser. Under no circumstances may any part of this book be photocopied for resale.

Cover design by Jessica Bell
Interior design by Amie McCracken and Jessica Bell

A catalogue record of this work is available from The National Library of Greece.

"Every time a font is stretched, a designer cries."

So I've heard.

TABLE OF CONTENTS

Introduction 18
Who Am I? 24
Why book cover design is so important, whether
self-published, indie, or traditionally published 26
    Space 40
    Avoid clutter 44
    Color 47
    Branding (for series or collections) 63
    Text and image synergy 73
    Working with an assistant .87
    DIY author designs vs. makeovers from professionals 91
Researching and choosing a book cover designer 95
Some of the biggest challenges an author and
a designer face during a collaboration 101
The balance between creating a book cover the author
loves, the designer loves, and a potential reader loves 106
How to prepare for a collaboration 110
    Front cover copy 111
    Back cover copy 116
    Distributor/printer and tech specifications 122
    Fancy features 129
How to ensure a smooth sailing collaboration 141
    Book a designer well in advance 141
    Will the designer read the entire manuscript? 142
    Email correspondence 144
    Phone correspondence 146
    Timeframe 147
    Design inspiration 147
    How things roll at Jessica Bell Design 149
Cost and recommended designers 154

A few last words (and connect with me!)	155
Acknowledgements	157
Appendix A: Attribution License	159
Appendix B: Project Agreement	160
Appendix C: Client Questionnaires	164
Appendix D: How to obtain puff quotes	169
Appendix E: How to obtain ISBNs	170
Appendix F: Popular trim sizes	171
Appendix G: Useful links	172
Appendix H: Binding options	173
Index of subjects and images	175

"*The Garden of Perfect Brightness* outsold *The Fragrant Concubine* for the first time ever last month!" said my client, Melissa Addey, after I redesigned the covers of her *Forbidden City* Series.

Figure 1

Figure 2

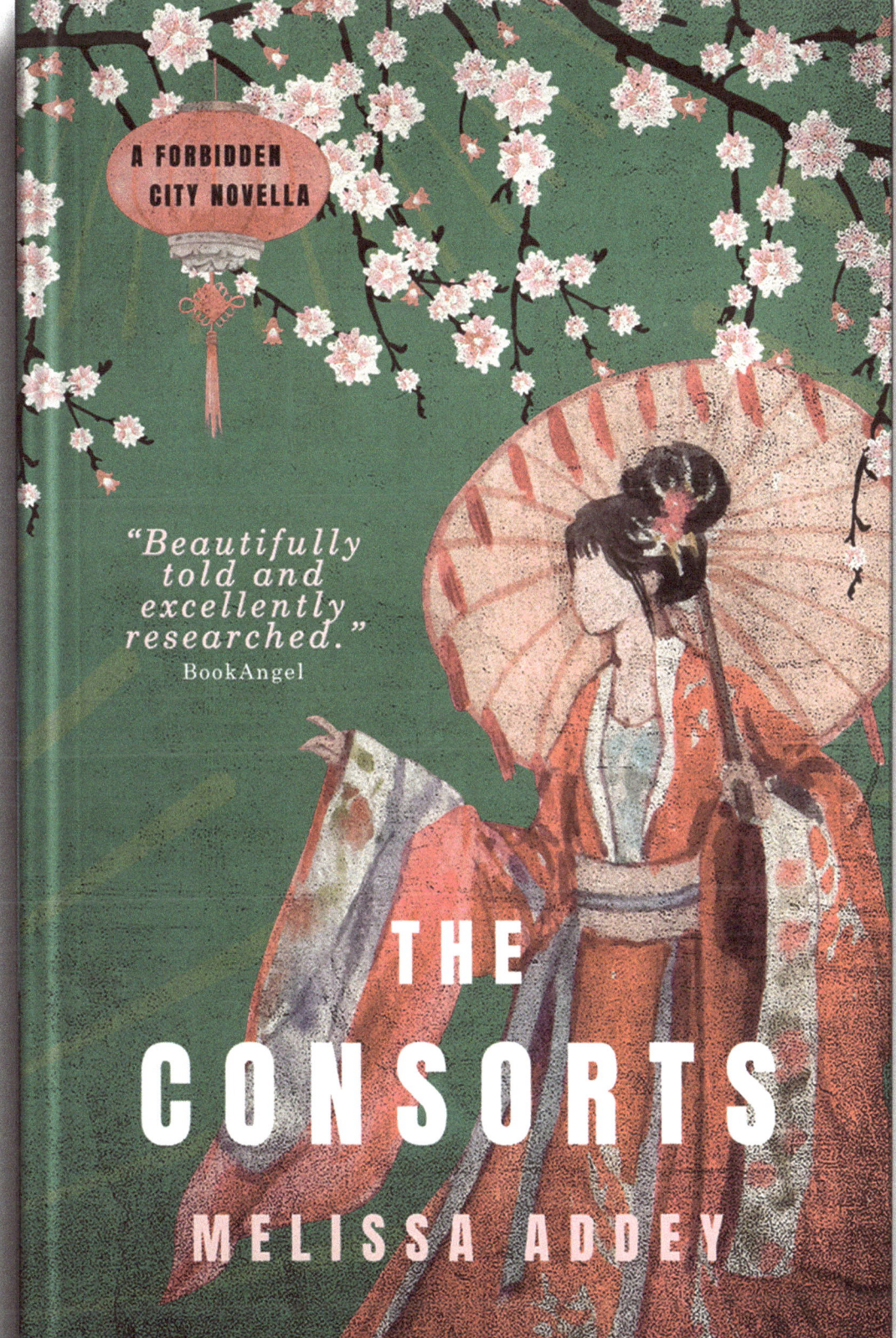

Figure 3

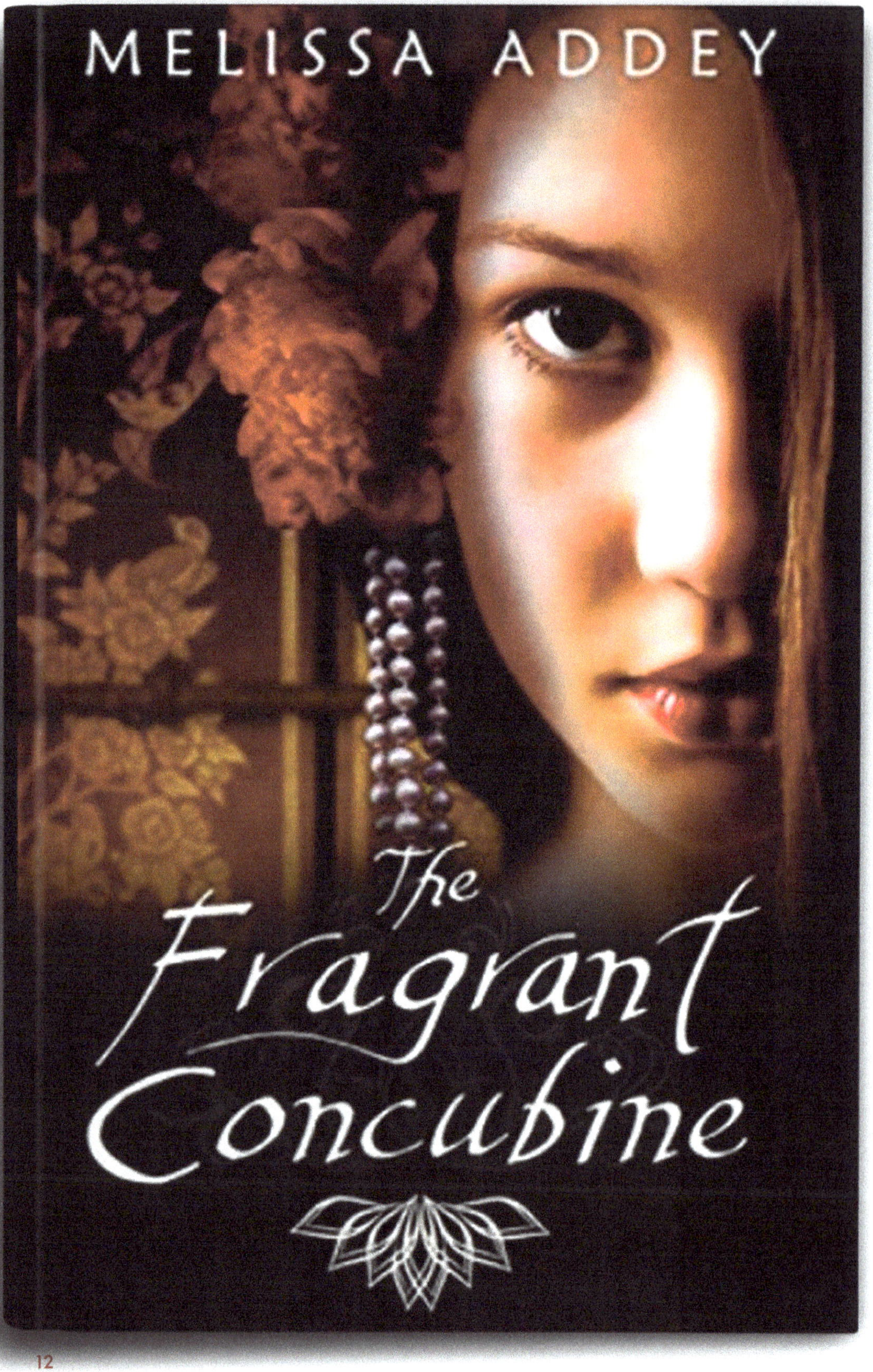

Figure 4

"Moving and wonderful."
Editor's Choice,
Historical Novel Society

A FORBIDDEN CITY NOVEL

THE FRAGRANT CONCUBINE

MELISSA ADDEY

Figure 5

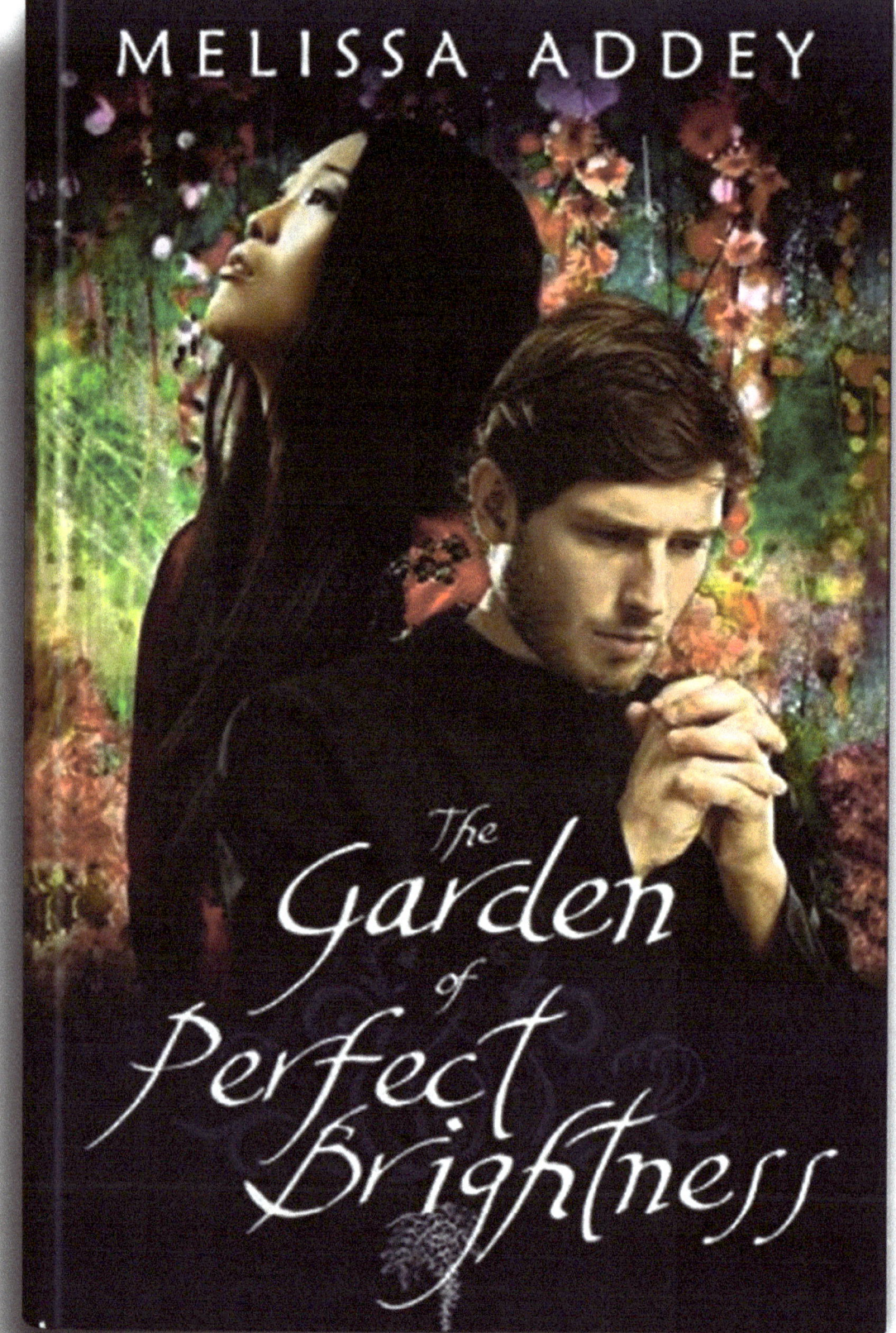

Figure 6

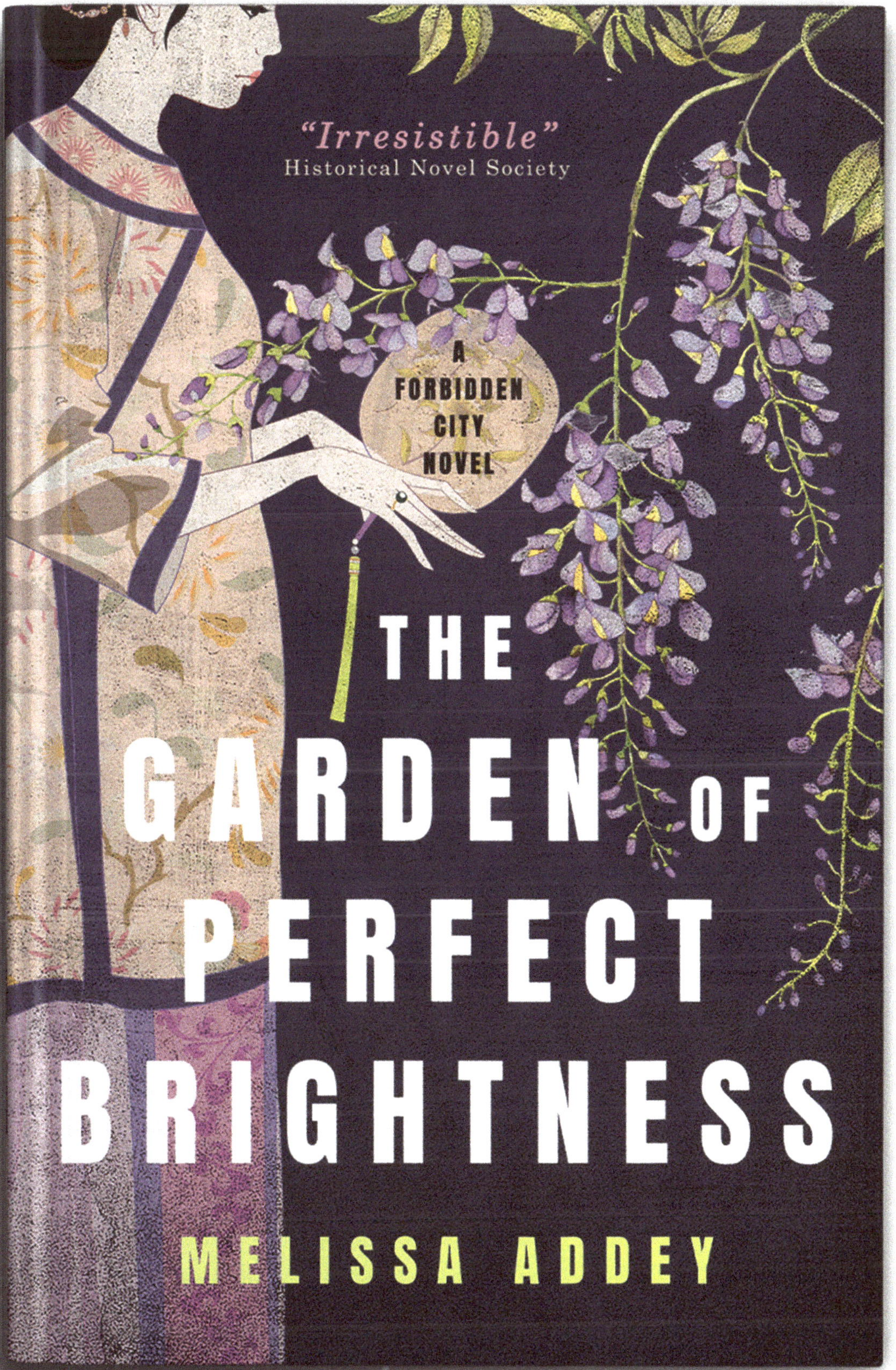

"Irresistible"
Historical Novel Society

A FORBIDDEN CITY NOVEL

THE GARDEN OF PERFECT BRIGHTNESS

MELISSA ADDEY

Figure 7

Figure 8

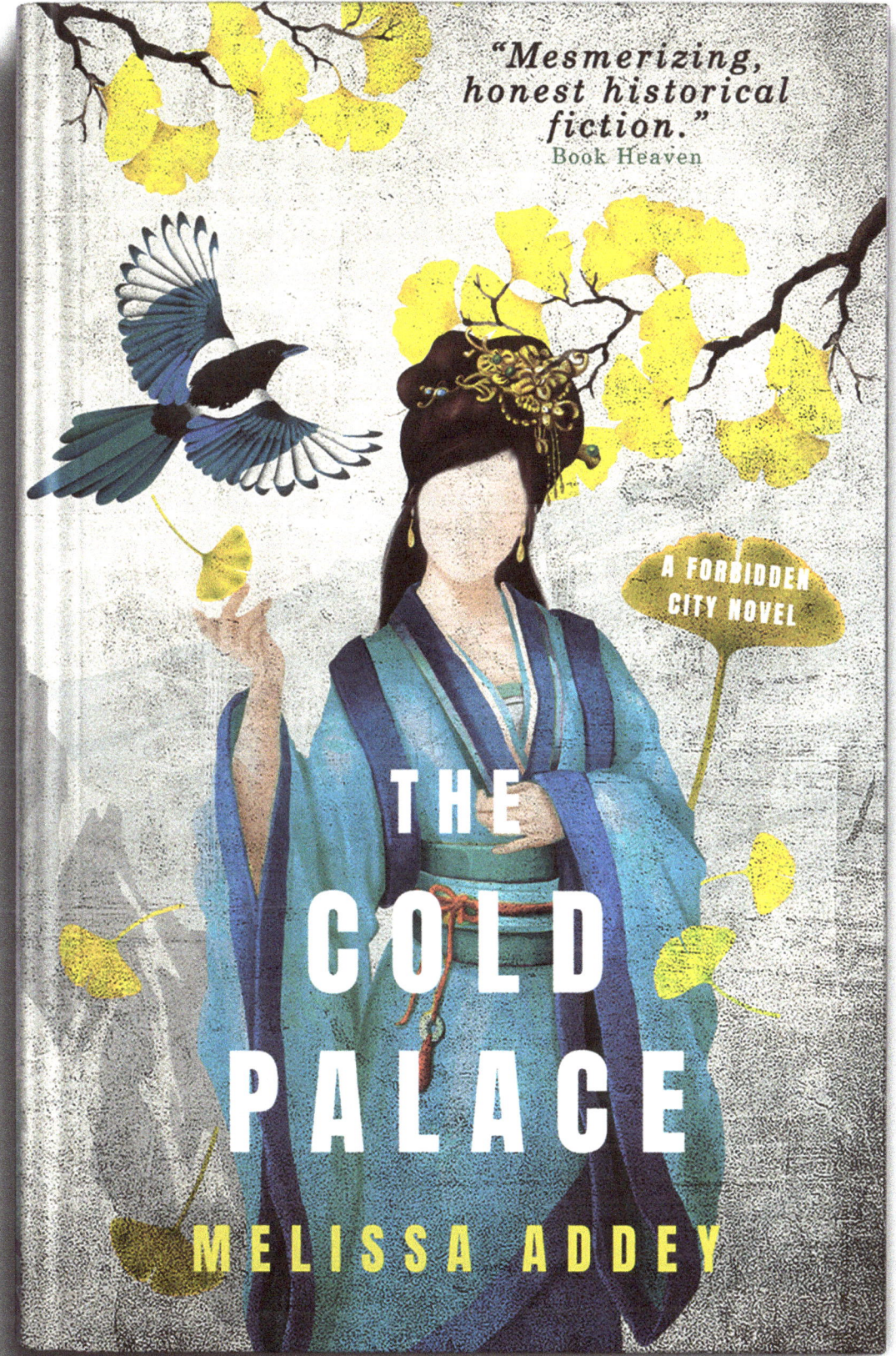

INTRODUCTION

Though I have written this book to educate the self-published author, it will also be useful if you're head of marketing or the graphics department at a publishing house, if you're studying graphic design and have dreams of designing book covers professionally, or if you are already a designer and you're looking for inspiration for workshops and classes. If you're reading this because of the latter, I simply ask for one little kindness: credit me and this book.

So, let's begin.

Great covers sell books. Bad covers do the opposite.

This is probably the first thing you need to tell yourself before making a mistake and publishing a book with a subpar cover. Don't have the budget? Then wait until you do. Because, trust me, publishing your book with a bad cover so that you can make money to buy a better cover DOES NOT WORK. Not to mention that this may sully your reputation. I have lost count of the times I've seen authors remorsefully admit defeat on social media, explaining why they've decided to discard their self-made covers and fork out the dosh for a professional design. These kinds of posts usually start with "I wish I would have known then what I know now." Hopefully this book will prevent this from happening to you.

This book is not about DIY book cover design. If you're looking for a tutorial on how to use Photoshop and design your own covers without first knowing what makes a book cover appealing to a reader, go ahead and swish on over to YouTube for some tutorials.

Though there is nothing wrong with designing your own covers (hell, I design my own!), knowing how to use Photoshop is not the place to start.

In order to do it well, you first need to understand how to create an eye-catching cover that is not only going to attract great praise from readers, but is most importantly, going to sell your books… TO READERS, not your friends. It's your ultimate marketing tool. Hate marketing? I bet you won't once you're finished reading.

I'm going to get stuck into the nitty gritty creative stuff like design elements that do/don't work and design trends in the marketplace, navigate the wishy-washy headspace of not being sure what you want, tell you how to organize the fundamental technical details that you may not know before commissioning a cover, show you how to get along like a house on fire with your designer (and find the *right* designer), and arm you with essential knowledge before you start learning how to design your own (if you ever want to).

Enjoy! Seriously, it's actually going to be fun.

"The jacket design is just right and draws one in … Trust me, I was a bookseller."

From a review of *Ever Rest* by Roz Morris

Figure 9 Cover design by Roz Morris, figure image copyright Owen Gent.

"I thought the cover was amazing and
made me want to read it."

From a review of *Arrows Tipped with Honey* by Jean Gill

Figure 10

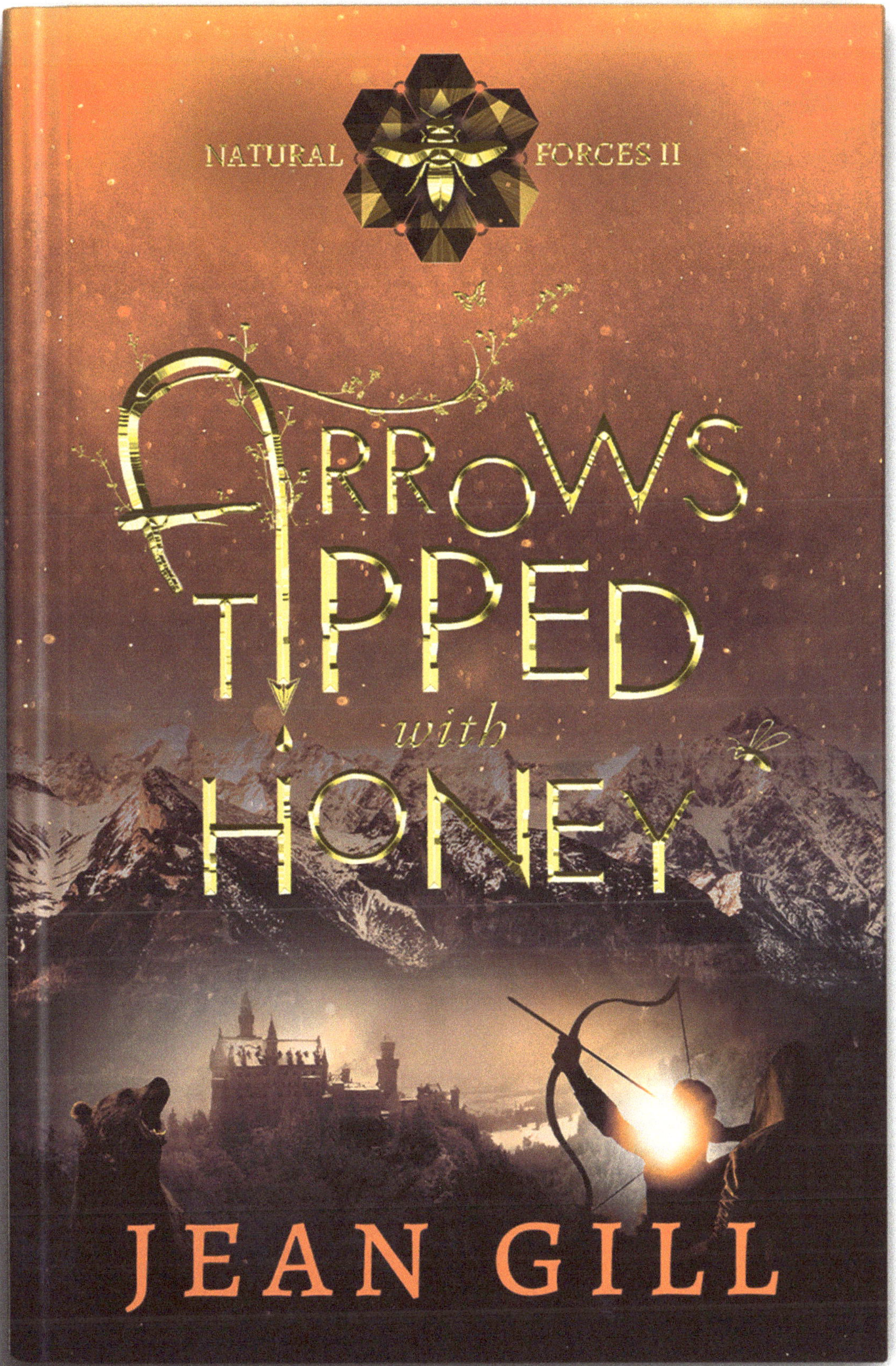

NATURAL FORCES II

Arrows Tipped with Honey

JEAN GILL

WHO AM I?

As a child of parents who are songwriters and musicians, and also artists in other ways such as dabbling in painting and drawing, I was singing before I could speak. Around the age of eleven, this turned into poetry writing, and then song writing, and playing piano and guitar. When I reached high school, I became extremely passionate about creative writing too. Already by sixteen I was writing short stories and at least one new song a week on my twelve-string guitar.

During my last year of high school, I had a strange obsession with graphic design. But as I was terrible at math, I failed my graphic design class, and didn't pursue it, because the school put a huge emphasis on graphic design leading into a career as an architect, and I just wanted to be creative. I was told to sign up for 'Art' class. All the meanwhile, my music was going strong, but my grades weren't perfect. All As and Bs in English and craft subjects, and mostly Ds in math and science, etc.

Those Ds meant I couldn't even get into my first choice of university course: Professional Writing at Deakin University, and I had to settle for Arts at Latrobe Bundoora (Victoria, Australia). At university, I majored in English and focused all my energy on my band. We were called spAnk, and we won some major competitions, got radio airplay, and appeared on TV. But then, I fell in love with a boy in Greece and moved here from Australia, leaving behind everything I had achieved music-wise by the time I'd turned twenty-two.

The responsibility of being an adult in a foreign country wasn't easy, so many of my first years were spent earning a living working in bars and restaurants. By the time I turned twenty-five, I had landed a job at a publishing company as an editor of English Language Teaching books, where I learned the ins and outs of editing, publishing, and eventually authoring ELT text books. I stayed in that career for eleven years. In my late twenties, I had the urge to write a novel. So, I did, sneaking in writing time before and after my day job. That novel was titled *String Bridge*, and was published in 2011 by a small press called Lucky Press. (Actually, the first novel I ever wrote ended up in the trash, but it did eventually lead to *String Bridge*!)

Unfortunately, just six months after its release the publishing company liquidated, and so I chose to self-publish it. This was the beginning of me becoming my own boss. I had the publishing and editing know-how, so I thought, why not try my hand at designing my own book covers, *and* start a literary journal?

Very soon after my design debut, I started designing covers for author friends as favors. I didn't charge back then, as it was just a fun way to make use of my creative energy. Until one of my friends told me I had talent, and that I should start a business. I took her advice, (thank you, Carol Cooper!) and since then I have designed hundreds of covers for indie, traditional, and hybrid authors, many of which have hit bestseller lists, and won awards. A few have even graced the shelves of WH Smiths at Heathrow airport.

Turns out that teacher in high school who told me to do 'Art' didn't know what-the-fff they were talking about because now, being a self-taught freelance graphic designer is how I earn a living. Designing book covers may be my main income, but I am still also writing books and music, and running my own publishing house, Vine Leaves Press.

Trust me yet?

WHY BOOK COVER DESIGN IS SO IMPORTANT, WHETHER SELF-PUBLISHED, INDIE, OR TRADITIONALLY PUBLISHED

Let me explain with a few hard-hitting anecdotes.

1. Have you ever had a friend ask you to read and review their book on your blog or website, but the cover is terribly designed, something they thought they'd just quickly whip up in Canva? And while you didn't have the heart to tell them that the title was indecipherable above the multicolored photo of a crowded farmer's market in Marrakesh, you still cringed every time you looked at it. You even felt embarrassed when you had to post it on your blog with your *glowing* review because the cover just did not do the brilliant book justice?

I have.

2. Has a friend ever given you a book and said, "It's brilliant, read it"? And has that book been sitting in your to-be-read pile for years because every time you pick it up and consider reading it, you look at the cover and for some reason change your mind?

I have.

3. Ever been so in love with a book cover that you couldn't resist buying the book? And when you read the book, it was nothing at all like you expected and you ended up disappointed even though it was technically a good read?

I have.

Now let's break down these three examples of unsuccessful book covers.

1. This example reflects an unattractive cover design that will put people off buying the book and will therefore miss out on a read that they might have thoroughly enjoyed.

2. In this example, there's nothing particularly wrong with the design, but there's nothing special about it either. Perhaps this book will be bought because of its reputation. But will it actually be read and reviewed? And if it's not read and reviewed, will those people ever buy this author's next book?

3. Wow. This sounds like a successful book cover design. This book has sold thousands of copies because the cover is so enticing. But there's a problem. All the review sites have lots of two and three-star ratings. And is this because the book was bad? Maybe not. But maybe the cover was giving a false impression of its contents. Maybe the cover showed steamy romance, but the romance ended up being a real-to-life domestic struggle to keep a marriage alive and avoided sex. Are you willing to jeopardize your reputation for income? Yes, sex sells, but think wisely. Because you may not be so lucky with your next book.

So, what's the collective moral of these stories? *Try to get it right the first time.*

The book's cover is the first thing a potential reader will typically see, even before reading the description. It's important because it's a reader's very first (and uninfluenced) impression of your book. Don't judge a book by its cover? Bollocks. This is the real world, and you want the book to sell. In this digital age, those first impressions could last as little as a split second as potential readers scroll down a webpage or social media profile. You need to catch their eye. Now. Dear writer, publisher, graphic artist, business person: first impressions always count. And they can *stain*.

That's not to say that there aren't exceptions. *Sometimes* you get a second chance. For example, my book String Bridge has been through the wringer.

The first cover was designed and illustrated by my then publisher. Then I got the rights back when they liquidated and I redesigned it myself. These were the early days back in 2012 when I'd just started messing around for fun. As you can see, the second and third covers are pretty dire. The last cover, which I designed in 2016, I still love, but it's not attracting many sales. It did a little better with each redesign, but nothing to shout about. And I honestly believe it's because it was not right from the very beginning. And I'm not sure I have it in me to give it another shot. It's time to leave that book in the past.

Figure 11 Cover design and illustration by Janice Phelps Williams

Figure 12

Figure 13

Figure 14

Sometimes, however, a cover reboot *will* revive a book, just like in Melissa Addey's case, which you saw at the beginning of the book. Also, there are covers out there that follow a tried and tested formula, that aren't particularly special in any way. I find that these kinds of covers are commonly used for genres that are binge-read, like romance, crime, and thriller.

Figures 15–18 (not designed by me) represent a very big trend for thrillers.

I can't tell you how tired I am of seeing shadowy silhouettes and bold lettering on thriller covers. But the trend works, and it catches the eye, so use it. But these trends only work until a new trend is born. By the time you read this book, the trend may be something different.

For example, since I started my career as a book cover designer, I've seen historical fiction covers with headless women (Figures 19–21), women walking away from the reader (Figures 22–24), and the bold and illustrated (Figures 25–27). These aren't my designs either and I've just sourced them from the internet.

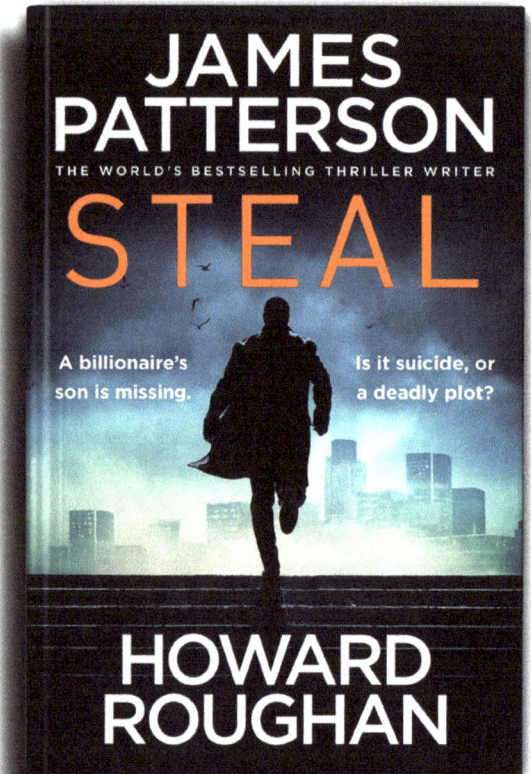
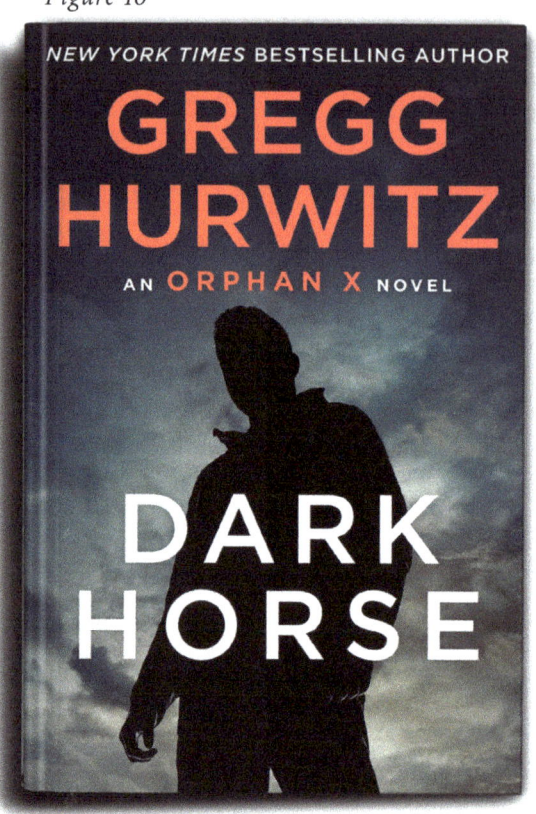

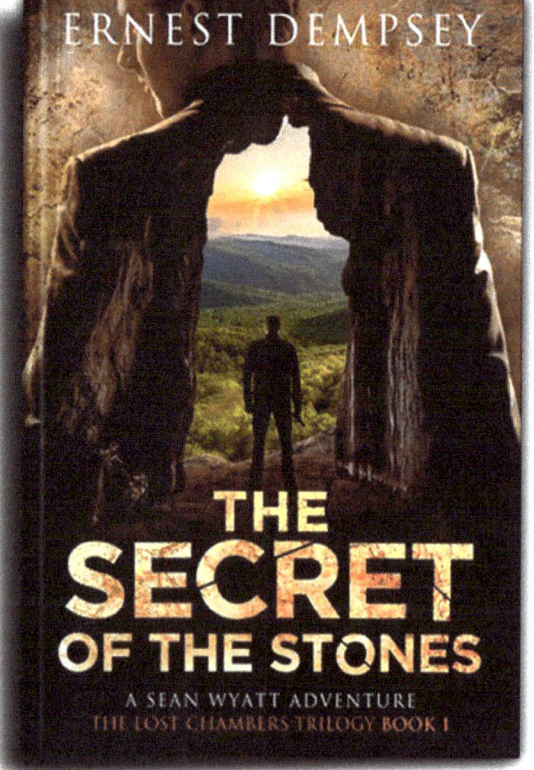

Figure 15 Figure 16

Figure 17 Figure 18

Figure 19

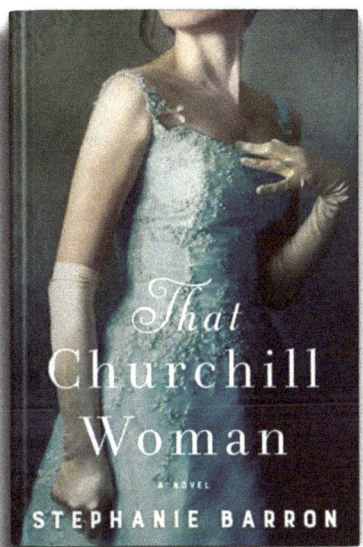

Figure 20

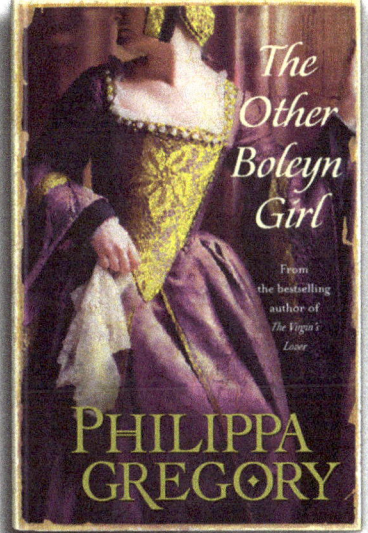

Figure 21

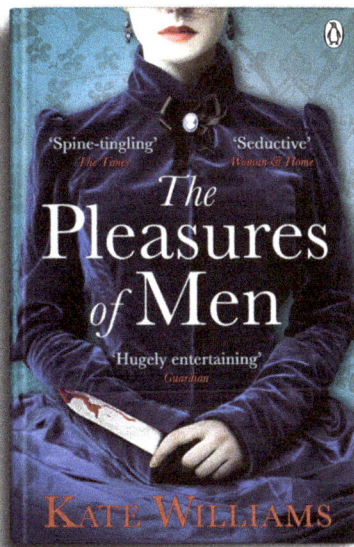

Figure 22

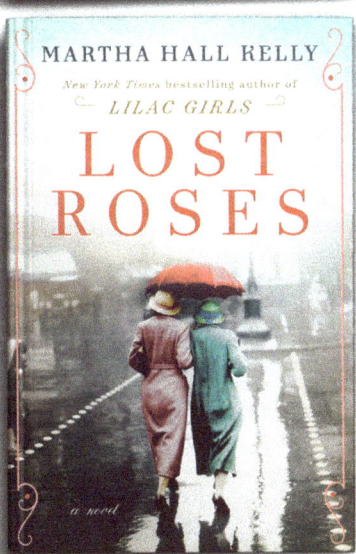

Figure 23

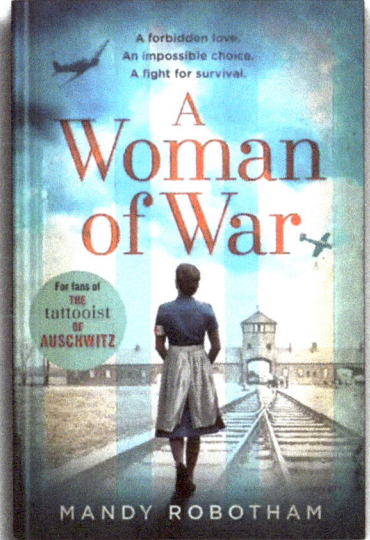

Figure 24

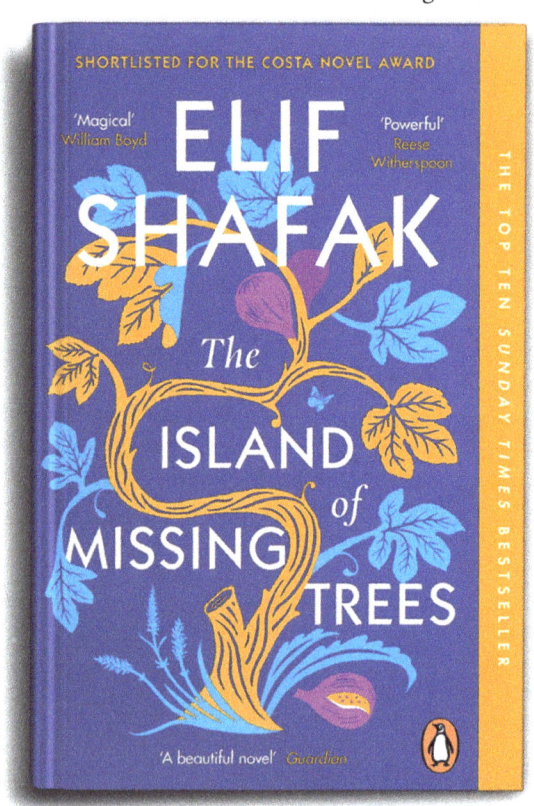

Figure 25

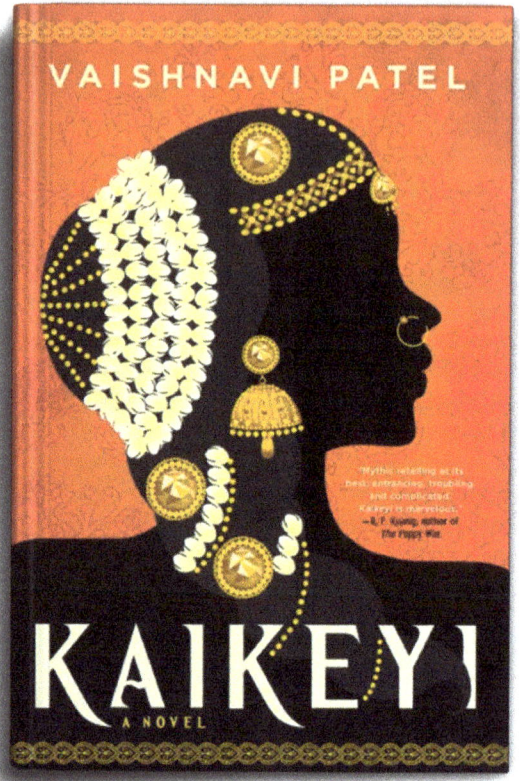

Figure 27

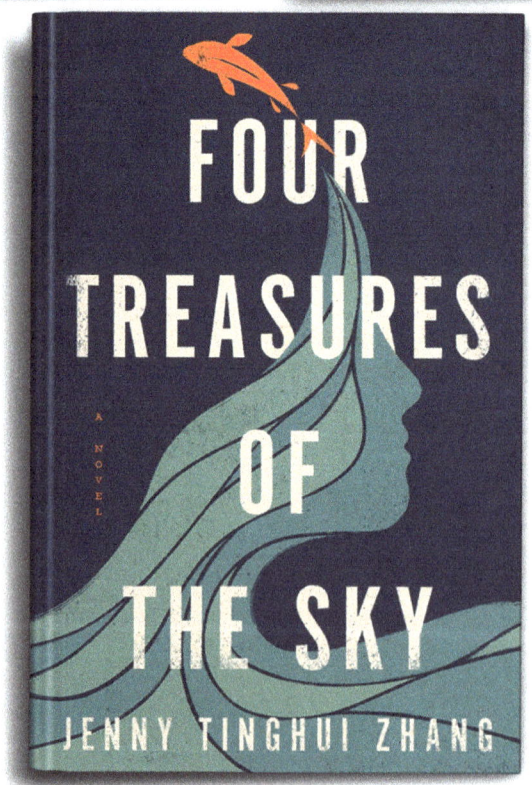

Figure 26

Maybe your book can be the catalyst of another trend?

Let's summarize. Why is a book cover so important?

Answer:
It sells your book, and might lead to a greater number of sales. Or, in the case of a bad cover, far fewer sales.

From reviews of *How Icasia Bloom Touched Happiness:*

"I was firstly drawn to this book by the beautiful cover …"

"I had to buy this book based on the cover alone. The story absolutely delivered on the cover's promise."

"First off, let's appreciate this stunning book cover! It caught my attention right away."

Figure 28

WHAT ARE THE ELEMENTS OF AN EYE-CATCHING, PROFESSIONAL COVER DESIGN?

The very first thing I'd like to mention is…

S   p   a   c   e

Not the one cluttered with galaxies of planets, stars and moons, but the one where you can walk into a room and not trip over the dog. A book cover with space allows the imagery and text to breathe. Utilizing space wisely will draw attention to the elements that you want potential readers to focus on.

Figure 29 is an example of nonfiction.

Figure 30 is an example of fiction.

And Figure 31 is an example of poetry in which I've taken an extreme perspective. Be sure to take a close look!

Figure 29

THE PROMISE OF PSYCHEDELICS

"TRULY VISIONARY, INSIGHTFUL, AND RELATABLE. A BRILLIANT MUST-READ!"
ROBERT ROGERS, *PSILOCYBIN MUSHROOMS: THE MYSTERY, SCIENCE AND RESEARCH*

DR. PETER SILVERSTONE

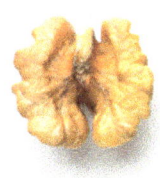 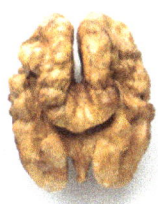 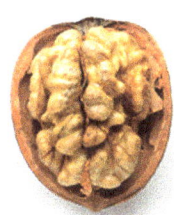 

Science-Based Hope for Better Mental Health

Figure 30

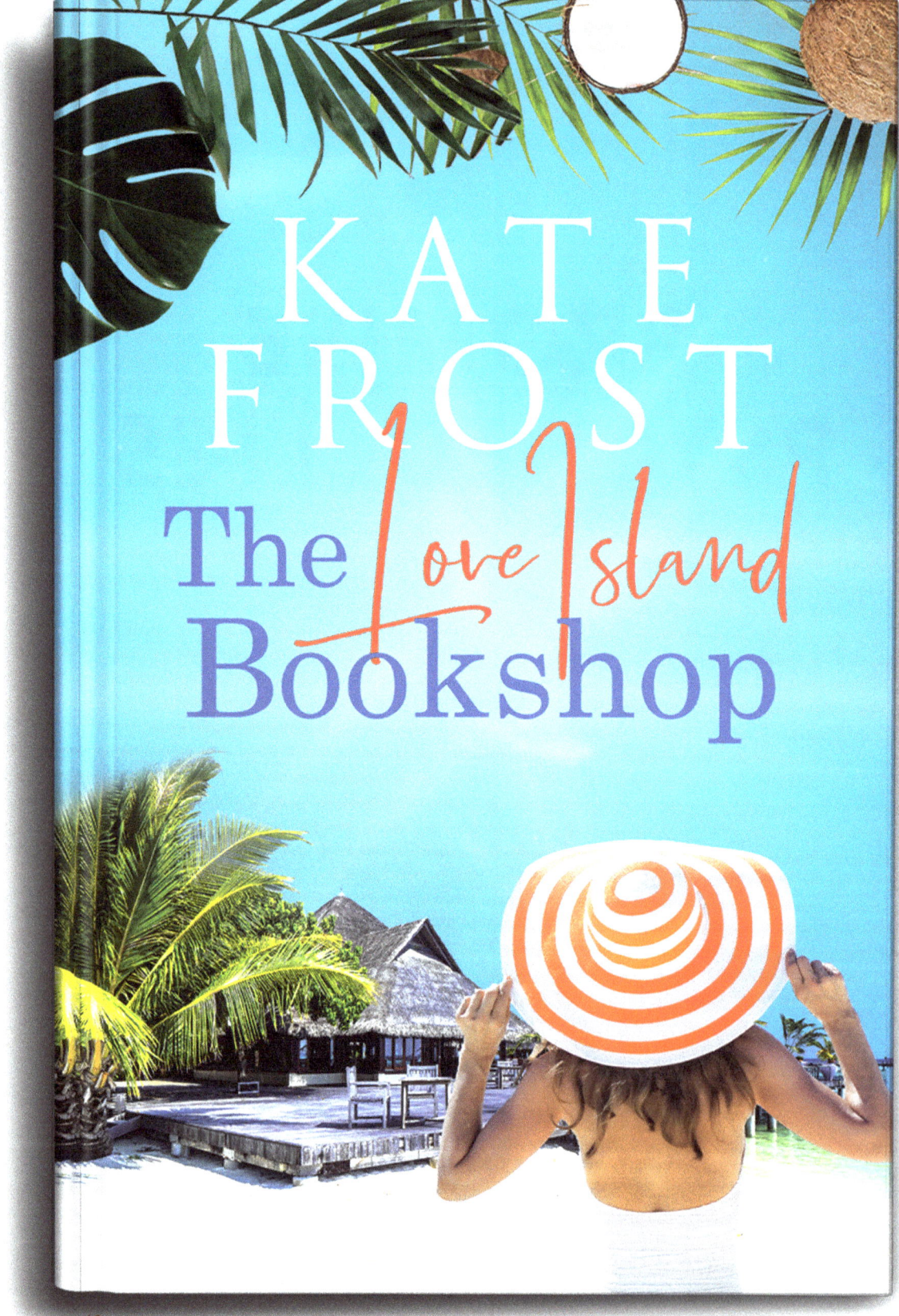

Figure 31

Michelle Robertson,
Hate Mail. Thank you for reading... |

Letters in verse

"Brilliantly spans the chasm between reporting the news and spinning fascinating tales."
Judy Walgren, Pulitzer Prize winner

As you can see in Figures 29–30, there is ample space for the text to breathe in the nonfiction and fiction covers, and the imagery is clear and telling. You know exactly what you're going to get with these books, and your eye is not wandering. The space used on the poetry cover, however, is used as reader bait. It's saying, "Hey can you read the title from there? Probably not. You'd better zoom in and check this out." It creates a little bit of mystery and intrigue.

Avoid clutter

As I'm sure you've noticed in the previous examples, it's very important not to clutter a cover. If there are too many elements fighting for attention, there is no focal point, and therefore nothing to attract the immediate attention of the eye. If you have a very talented and artistic cover designer, it's possible that strategic cluttering can work.

Have a look at Figure 32 as an example. I'm very proud of this one.

Here, I've pretty much filled in all available space with either text or illustration. But it's still easy to read and understand what's going on. This is due to the use of color. The various colors allow us to distinguish between the elements so I've been able to get away with this kind of "clutter."

But please don't try to fit all your story elements in, like in Figure 33. Not mine!

Figure 32

"GLOWS WITH AUTHENTICITY"
GISH JEN, *THE RESISTERS*

TRUTH *like* **OIL** CONNIE BIEWALD

"EXPLORES RACE, IDENTITY, PREJUDICE, COMMUNITY AND SECRETS. EMOTIONALLY TRUE AND BEAUTIFULLY WRITTEN"
ROBIN FARMER, *MALCOLM AND ME*

Truth Like Oil, is the impactful story of two mothers in Boston, Massachusetts: Nadine Antoine, a Haitian-American nurses' aide, and Hazel Watkins, a white cantankerous nonagenarian felled by a stroke who struggles with her own helplessness and dependency.

When Nadine's youngest son, Chance, is arrested and her eldest son, Henry, the only Black undergraduate on a scholarship at his college, threatens to quit to help the family, Nadine wrestles with how much of her sons' parentage she is willing to reveal to her boys.

Meanwhile, Chance's basketball coach, Gary, who is also Hazel's spoiled and neglectful son, turns up in court to defend the boy. Suddenly, while fighting for her sons' futures, Nadine must contend with Gary's intentions and his romantic overtures.

Polyphonic and vibrant, *Truth Like Oil* is a brilliant tale of racial bias and the foundations of community, a novel of our times and totally irresistible.

"FULL OF WISDOM AND COMPASSION, THIS EMOTIONALLY BOUNTIFUL NOVEL IS ... BIG-HEARTED AND INTELLIGENT"
LAURA BROWN, *MADE BY MARY* AND *QUICKENING*

FICTION
vineleavespress.com
ISBN 978-1-925965-50-6

Figure 33

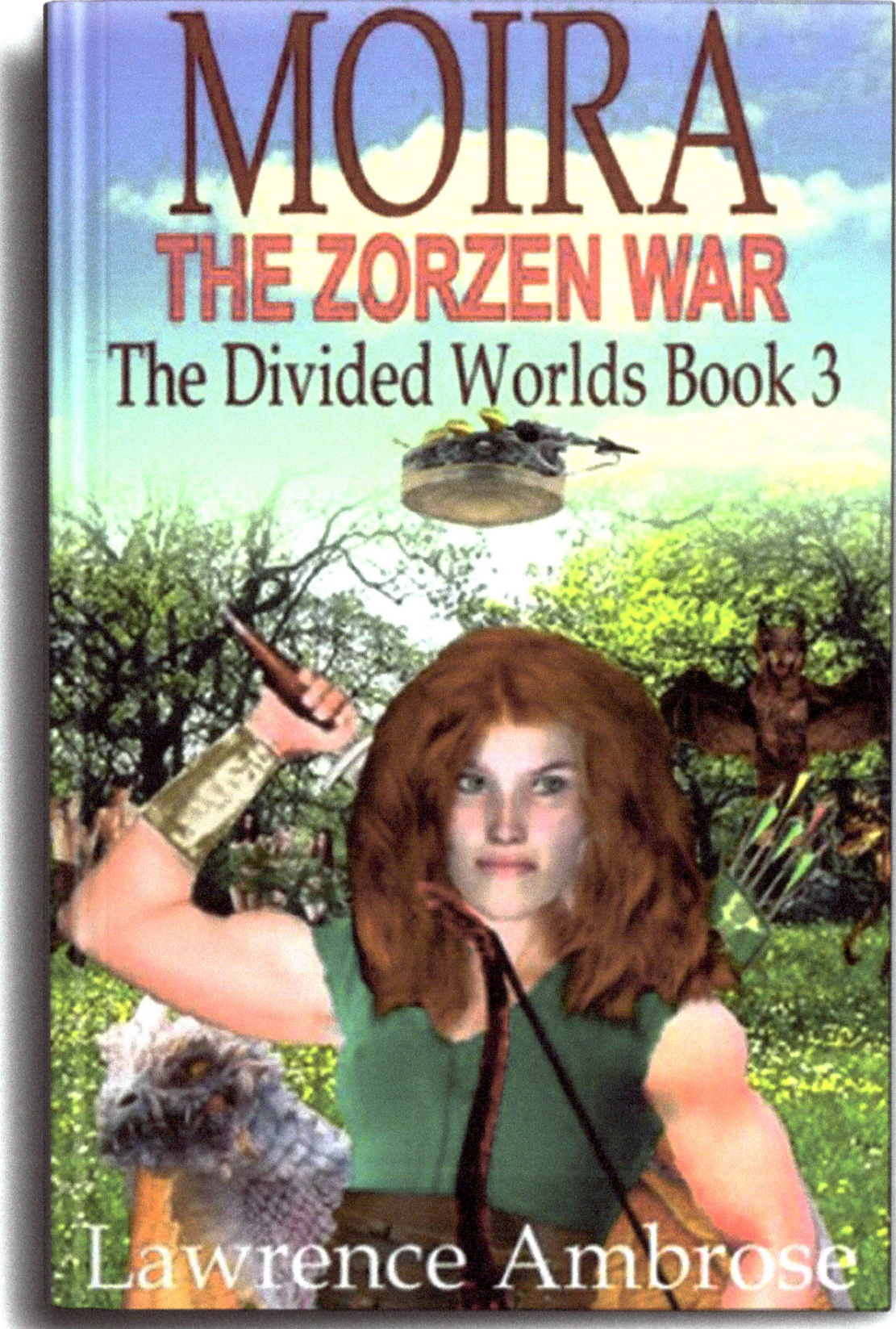

Color

Too many different colors on a cover can get a bit confusing for the eye. Just like with the space issue, too many colors can cause a cluttering effect. This is because colors help separate the elements on the cover, as well as draw attention to specific elements on a cover. I typically try not to exceed three main colors and two accent colors. In the covers labeled Figure 34, 35 and 36, I've kept to very few for maximum effect.

Of course, this strategy doesn't work for every genre or idea (especially when using photography), but it's good to keep in mind that too many colors may draw readers away rather than in.

If you take a look at the color chart in Figure 37, you'll see that there are common complimentary color combinations. These combinations are a good place to start if you are trying to decide on a color scheme for your cover. If you want to make some more advanced selections, check out Adobe's color wheel online.

Refer to Appendix G for the direct URL.

Figure 34

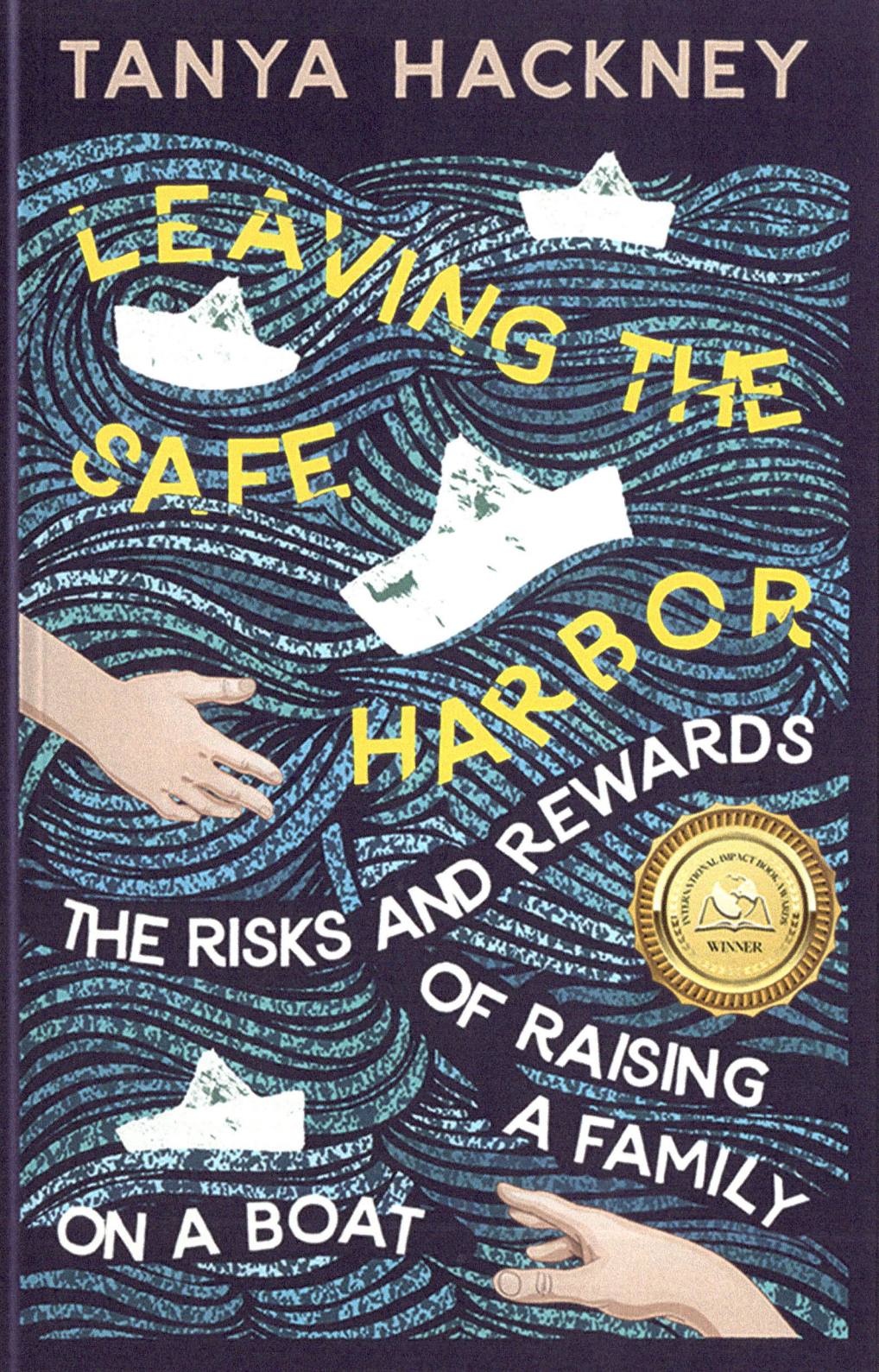

Figure 35

Figure 36

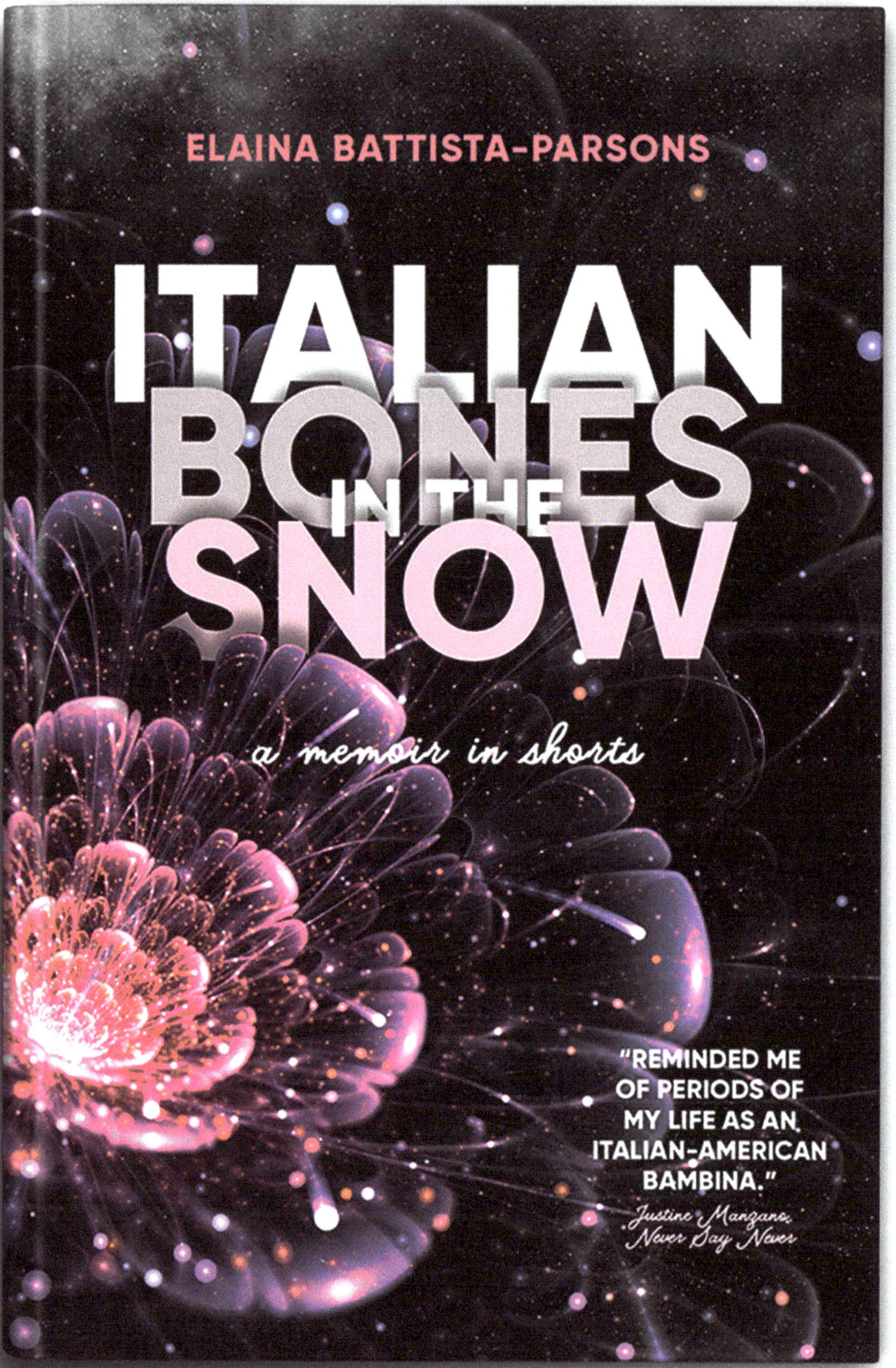

Figure 37

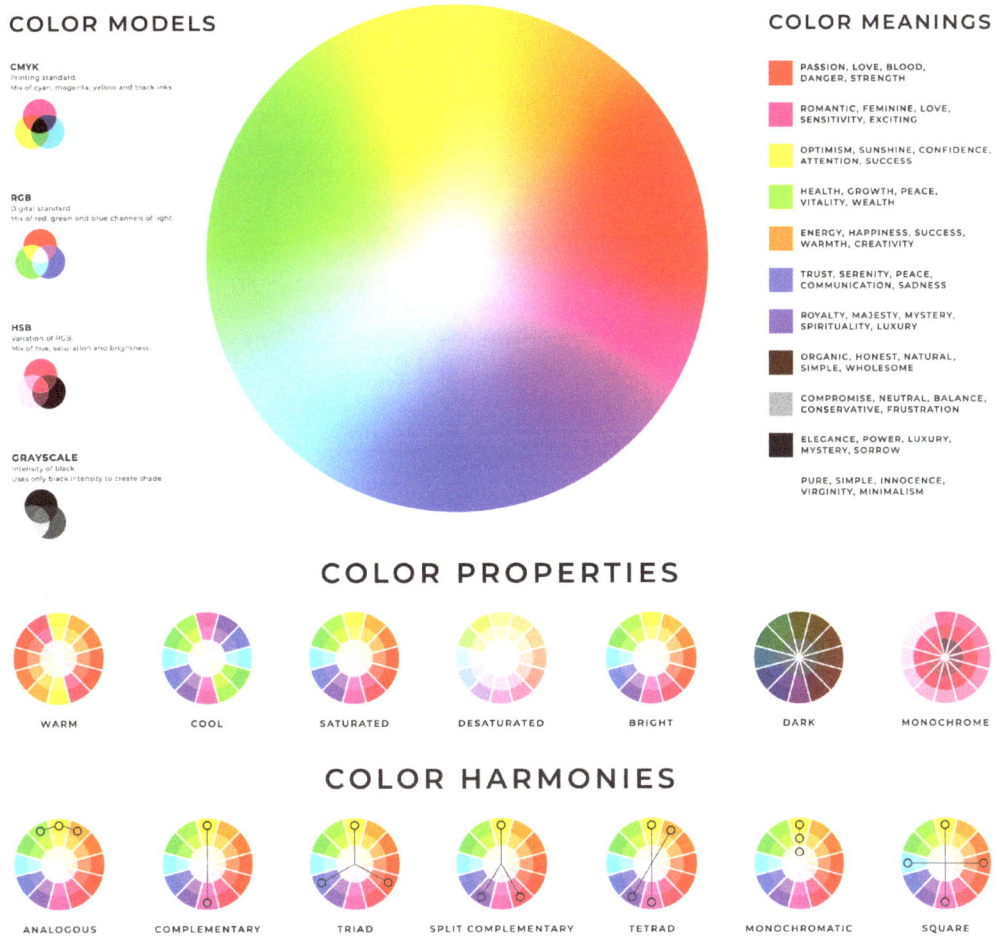

Similarly, color plays a huge role in how a cover affects us emotionally. I find that I gravitate toward purple and turquoise for their sense of calm, blues/greens with yellows/oranges/reds for their air of confidence and reliability, and contrasty color combos like red, black and yellow/white, which not only draw the eye, but really do scream, "Hey, I know what I'm talkin' 'bout!"

Take a look at Figure 38 for a list of common colors and their meanings.

Figure 38

TEAL	BLUE	INDIGO	VIOLET	MAGENTA	BEIGE
Communication	Stability	Devotion	Spirituality	Compassion	Flexible
Self-sufficiency	Loyalty	Justice	Imagination	Co-operation	Dependable
Sophistication	Confidence	Wisdom	Wisdom	Self respect	Reliable
Freedom	Cold	Spirituality	Luxury	Inspiration	Familiar
Trust	Responsibility	Relaxation	Compassion	Creativity	Neutral
	Honesty		Sensitivity	Luxury	
	Trust		Mystery	Intuition	
	Security			Fascination	
	Relaxation			Motivation	
	Calm				
	Authority				

GREEN	CYAN	PURPLE	LAVENDER	PINK	BROWN
Nature	Emotional balance	Luxury	Youth	Romance	Warmth
Life	Friendship	Ambition	Vitality	Compassion	Foundation
Safety	Good luck	Independence	Mystery	Love	Nature
Jealous	Self expression	Mystery	Spiritual	Immature	Earthly
Proceed	Wisdom	Imagination	Sensitive	Playful	Security
Growth	Joy	Spiritual	Magic	Admiration	Familiarity
Harmony	Trust	Compassion	Nature	Energy	
Stability	Productive	Sensitive		Action	
Balance		Inspiration		Creativity	
Relax		Power			
Encourage		Intuition			
Possess					

BLACK	SILVER	MAROON	RED	ORANGE	AMBER
Elegance	Glamour	Ambition	Romance	Warmth	Warmth
Power	Grace	Creativity	Sensitivity	Abundance	Energy
Control	Formal	Excitement	Leadership	Determination	Positivity
Authority	Composure	Strength	Willpower	Success	Happiness
Evil	Minor Wealth		Danger	Optimism	Creativity
Death	Metallic Finish		Energy	Adventurous	Progress
Discipline	Technology		Passion	Creativity	
Intimidation			Courage	Fun	
Fear			Attention	Stimulation	
Mystery			Urgency	Attention	
Hidden feelings			Caution	Freedom	
			Warning	Fascination	
			Warmth		

GREY	WHITE	BURGUNDY	CORAL	GOLD	YELLOW
Emotionless	Innocence	Sophistication	Self-love	Compassion	Joy
Conservative	Safety	Power	Creativity	Courage	Positivity
Neutral	Illumination	Influence	Balance	Magic	Vigor
Formal	Perfection			Wisdom	Remembrance
Quiet	Purity			Wealth	Intellect
Depress	Fresh start			Success	Enthusiasm
Timeless	Neutral			Money	Opportunity
Composure				Heritage	Spontaneous
Maturity					Positivity
					Energy

If you're familiar with advertising tactics, you'll know that color is used strategically in product packaging and business logos. For a more robust list with deeper explanations, just search online for "color symbolism" and the color you are looking for.

Nonfiction

If you write nonfiction, color symbolism should play a huge role in deciding on your cover design and color scheme. Have a look at the following nonfiction covers that I designed where color symbolism is paramount:

In *Dying with Dad* (Figure 39), I've used turquoise and pink. Turquoise represents emotional balance, wisdom, spiritual grounding, patience, intuition, and more. Pink represents universal love of oneself and of others, inner peace, acceptance, contentment, and more.

In *Choices* (Figure 40), I've used a lavender shade of purple. This color combines the calm stability of blue and the fierce energy of red, wisdom, dignity, pride, independence, youth, vitality, and more.

In *Mom on Wheels* (Figure 41), I've used red. Red is linked to the most primitive physical, emotional, and financial needs of survival and self-preservation, leadership, willpower, courage, determination, and more.

Figure 39

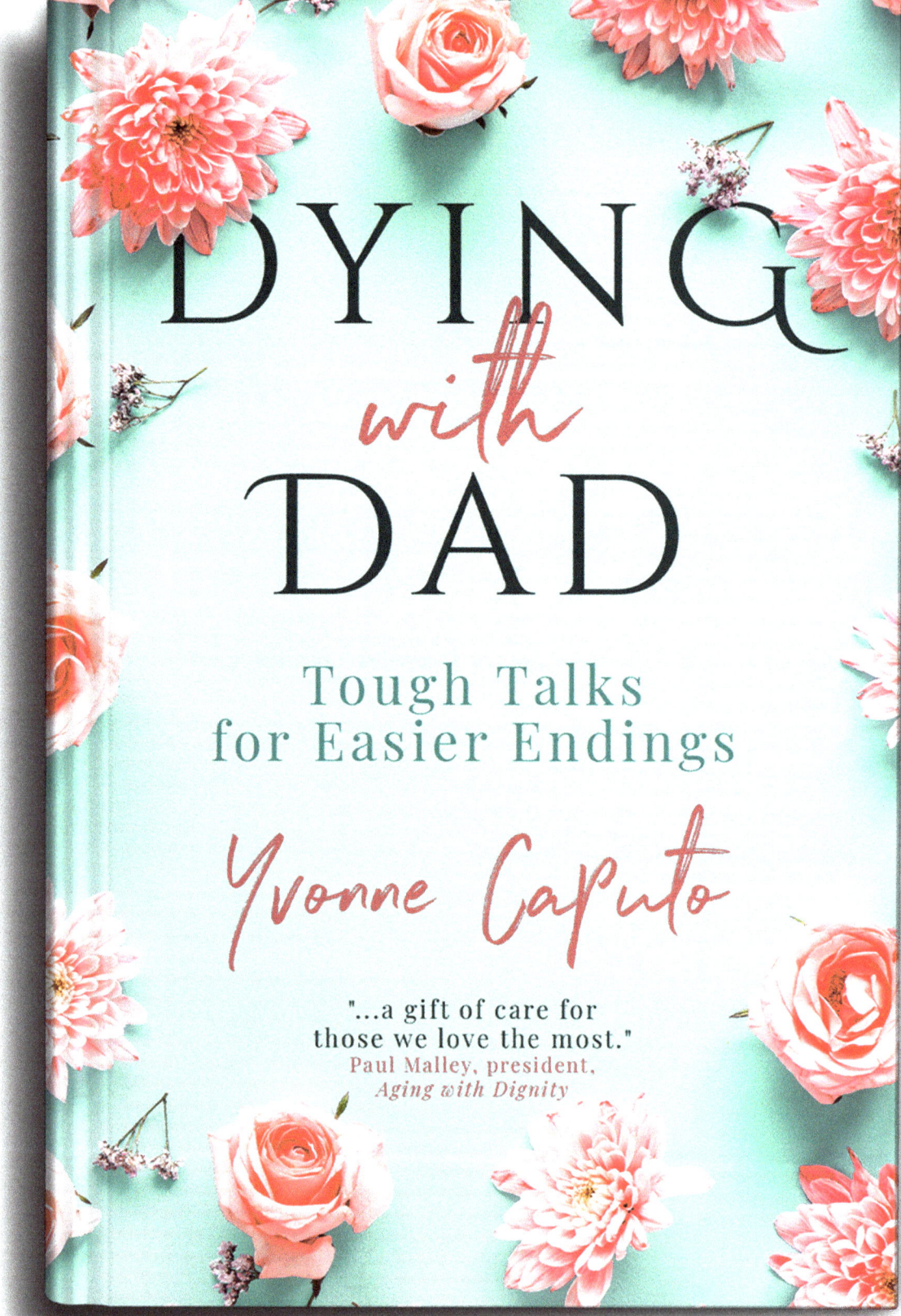

Figure 40

Figure 41

"EMPOWERING AND PRACTICAL."
THE HONOURABLE CHANTAL PETITCLERC,
PARALYMPIAN, SENATOR, AND MOTHER

MARJORIE AUNOS, PHD

MOM ON WHEELS

THE POWER OF PURPOSE FOR A PARENT WITH PARAPLEGIA

Fiction

You can also use this color strategy for fiction if your book is heavily themed and contains symbolism that drives your story.

For example, my novel, *Bitter Like Orange Peel*, really screamed for an orange cover. But I did experience quite a conundrum, because thematically, the book is quite dark. In the book, I use a wilting orange tree to symbolize a gradual breakdown of familial warmth, so I needed to juxtapose the "warmth" of the orange. On both versions of the cover (yes, I made two!) I decided to use orange, black, and gray. Orange represented warmth, determination, freedom, and fascination. I used black and gray to represent the elements of fear, hidden feelings, depression and emotionlessness. If you take a look at Figure 38 again, and at the blurb of the novel, you'll understand completely what I was getting at by using these colors.

I also want to mention quickly, why I have two versions of this cover: because I made the rookie mistake that I illustrate in anecdote three from section one! Go check out the reviews of this book on Goodreads. This book is my biggest failed success. The first cover drew a very big young adult crowd, and the book is *so* not YA. In fact, it's something quite the opposite of what young adult readers would ever enjoy. Also, please don't judge these covers too harshly. I designed them in 2013 and 2016! They are okay, but they aren't my current standard of great.

Have a look at Figures 42 and 43 for the two covers.

Figure 42

Figure 43

the bell collection: beautiful ugly words

bitter
like
orange
peel

a novel

jessica
bell

Poetry

We mustn't forget about poetry.

I have always felt that poetry is a unique mix of fiction and nonfiction. Poets tend to pour their hearts and souls into their work, even if the literal outcome is not "real." I know that I do. But the journey toward that result is always very real. It certainly is for me. We wear our metaphors on our sleeves. So yes, color symbolism in poetry for the win.

Figures 44 and 45 show a couple of poetry covers in my portfolio that I adore. Check out the color meanings in Figure 38, and the book blurbs online, and see if you can identify the symbolism used in each.

If you don't think color symbolism is relevant for your work, simply use it for fun!

Figure 44

Figure 45

Branding (for series or collections)

As you probably know, if you're writing a series, or want to create a linked collection of books, the covers need to be cohesive in some way. This is not just a pretty design preference. It actually helps readers recognize (and purchase) the books. Of course, every series or collection of books is going to need a design specific to the content, but here are some general ideas that can be implemented:

1. Font and text placement
2. Image structure and layout
3. Series logo or emblem/symbol

Figures 46–57 are examples of one series, one collection, and one series using a recurring symbol.

If you're wondering what the difference between a series and a collection is, a series refers to a series of books that must be read in order, from book one, to comprehend the story. A collection refers to a group of standalone books that the author or publisher wishes to link by creating an author brand or thematic visuals, usually for marketing purposes. Check out the evolution of book covers for Jeanette Winterson's books as a great example. A simple internet search will bring them up.

Figure 46   Figure 47

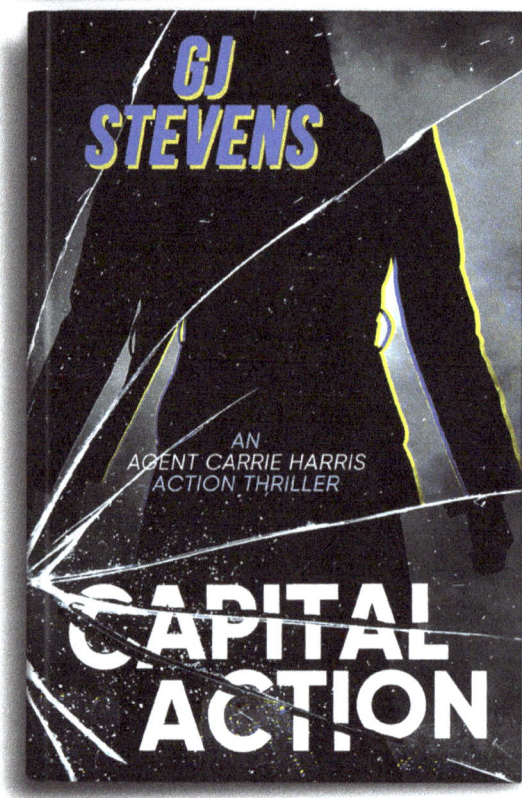
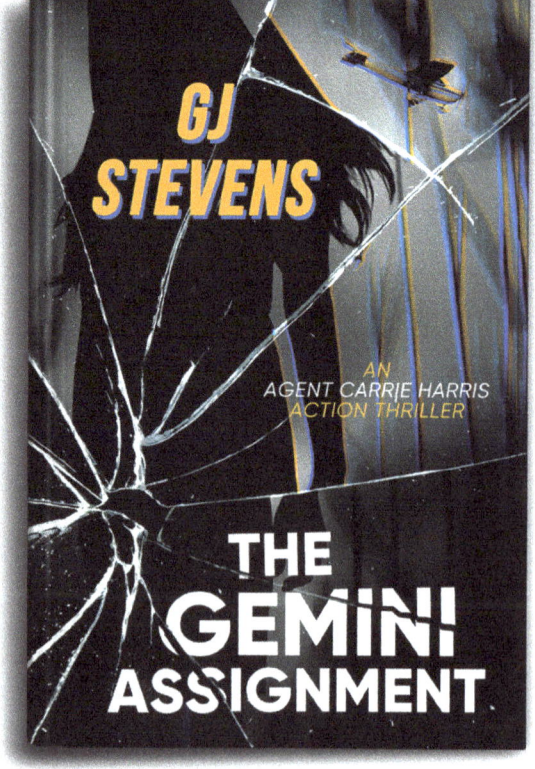

Figure 48   Figure 49

Figure 50   Figure 51

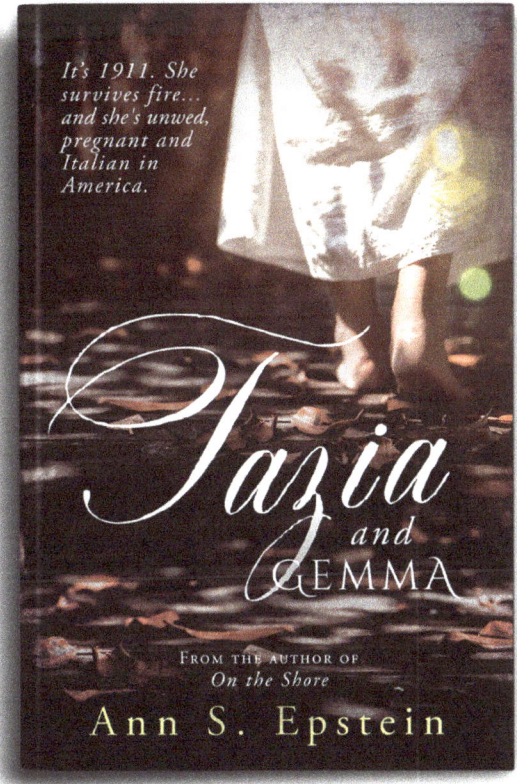

Figure 52   Figure 53

Figure 54   Figure 55

Figure 56   Figure 57

Once you have a good collection of books, you also might want to think about doing a boxed set using the branding you have established with the individual covers. These can be both digital and physical, but can still come in various forms.

Digital can come as a 3D boxed set (or "box set" which is often used, but that's grammatically incorrect) which everyone has come to expect, or as a 2D cover, the way a typical eBook cover would look. The physical can come as an all-in-one paperback or hardcover edition. Have a look at *The Forbidden City* Series by Melissa Addey (Figures 58–60).

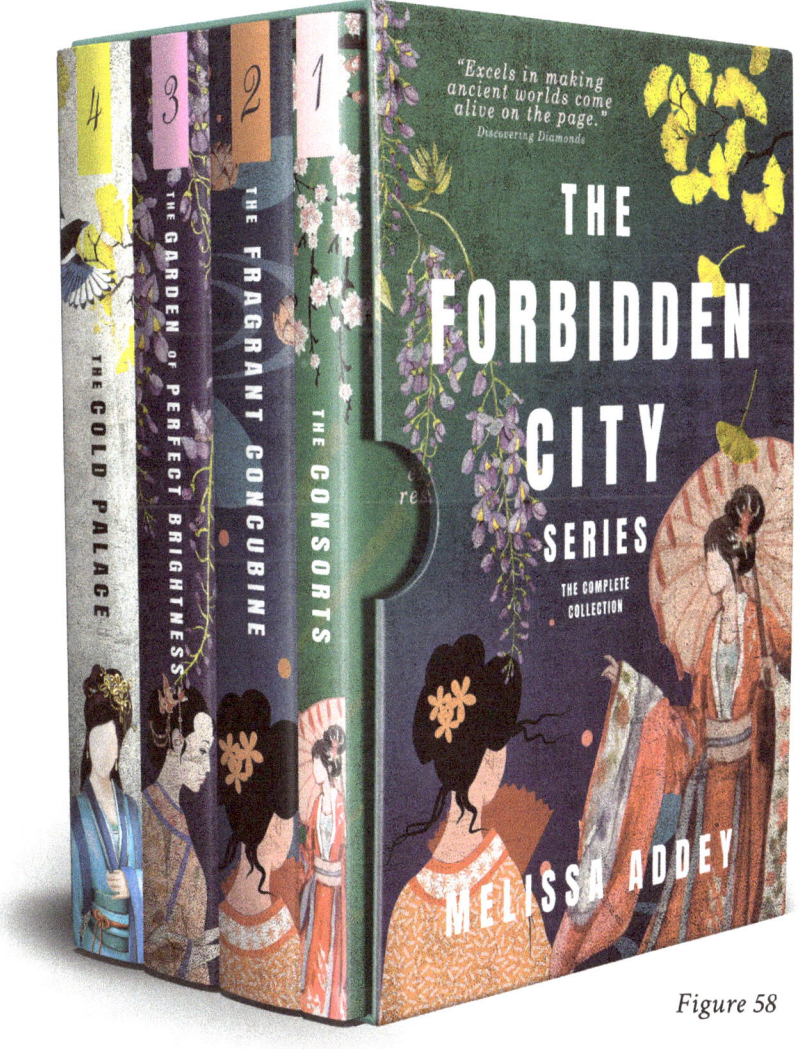

Figure 58

Figure 59

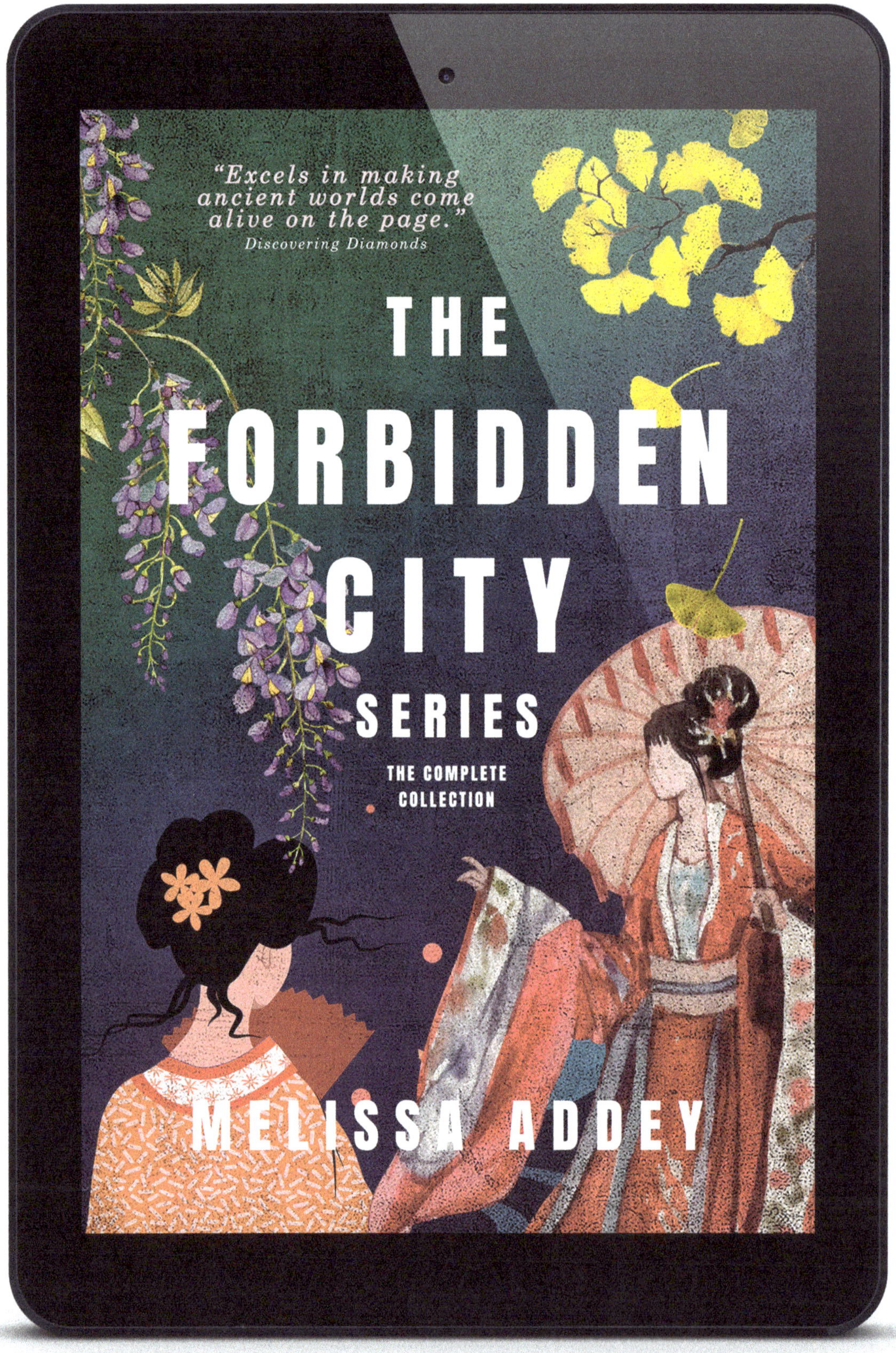

Figure 60

If you want to go all fancy-pants, you could even have a real boxed set of books in an actual physical box designed.

Or go all out and get a completely new design made to drum up some new interest, like my client Jean Gill did for her Natural Forces trilogy. Think of it as a special edition and you could create a whole new marketing campaign around it giving your series a new life and maybe even new readers. Have a look at Figure 61.

If you're thinking about branding yourself as an author and having a publishing logo designed for your barcode area and book spines, a good place to start is with color symbolism, i.e. what does your business represent? I won't go into the complexities of logo design here, since this is a book about book cover design, but if you have a look at Appendix C, you'll see the questionnaire my logo clients receive, which serves me as a design brief. The questions might help you figure out what you are all about as a publisher too.

You can see a few examples of logos I've designed in Figure 62.

Figure 61

Figure 62

Text and image synergy

Sometimes font choice is the only thing standing between a successful vs. failed cover design because the imagery might actually be worth keeping.

A good designer will know exactly what style of font suits your design and genre, so it's not really something you should concern yourself with if you don't intend to design your covers by yourself. But I'm pretty sure you've seen covers on which you just "know" the font is not working with the imagery and it makes it look amateurish.

Have you ever heard indie authors laughing and joking about Papyrus, and how it screams amateur? It's been labeled "the king of bad fonts." I agree. It doesn't look good on anything. A simple internet search will bring it up for you to see. There are a few other fonts you should avoid if you want to be taken seriously, and those are: Comic Sans, Bradley Hand, Mistral, and Chiller. These are the five serious offenders in my opinion, but if you search for "fonts to never use on a book cover" you'll find many more offenders and opinions about them.

You also need to consider the placement of the text. A good cover designer will design imagery and text simultaneously so that they complement each other and seamlessly combine with each other. This is why it's a challenge (and usually more expensive) to approach a designer with a ready image or illustration that was not originally produced by someone who is familiar with book cover design.

> *Client:* **I have a photograph that will create the cover image for us which will cut down the work for us. With that in mind, how much would you then charge me to plug everything together and add the author bio, headshot, title on front cover and spine, etc.?**

You cannot just grab an image and slap text on top of it. Well, you can, but the result will more often than not resemble something an author put together quickly on Canva, which unfortunately screams all the negative things people have to say about self-published books. (And some small presses too!) You need to compete with all the traditional publishers who have huge budgets to play with, and all the authors who believe you are ruining their reputation because you decided to take shortcuts and skimp on quality.

I'm going to show you an illustration I was once given to produce a book cover for an "old American comic book sci-fi/fantasy manga mix graphic novel."

Before moving forward, I need to comment on the "genre" here. As a designer, it's not really my place to be offering advice on book content (though I could since I'm an author and a publisher too), but it *is* my place to be commenting on target audience. Genre *leads* to target audience and target audience leads to *design*. For this project, I had no say about any design elements (I'll get to that in a moment), but if I had, where was I supposed to start? Old American comic? Sci-fi/Fantasy? (Even those two can differ drastically.) Manga? There's absolutely nothing wrong with writing multi-genre books. *I* write multi-genre books. But choices need to be made regarding who you intend to market the book to. Of course, it can end up reaching a wide range of audiences, but it also needs to *start* somewhere solid first.

Authors tend to forget the key word in *target* audience. The arrow cannot hit more than one circle with one shot.

Back to the illustration. Take a look at Figure 63.

Figure 63 Illustration by Aaron Lopresti

The author asked me to not alter it, since he'd paid for it to be illustrated specifically for the book and it also depicted a vital scene from the book (more about trying to shoehorn story elements in later). I began to get heart palpitations. I wasn't sure I was going to be able to put text on this thing and make it look good, and most of all, make it readable. I very reluctantly took the project on, rolled up my sleeves, so to speak, and tried to look at it as a challenge. Figures 64–66 are the three samples I came up with.

Figure 64

Can You Make the Title Bigga?

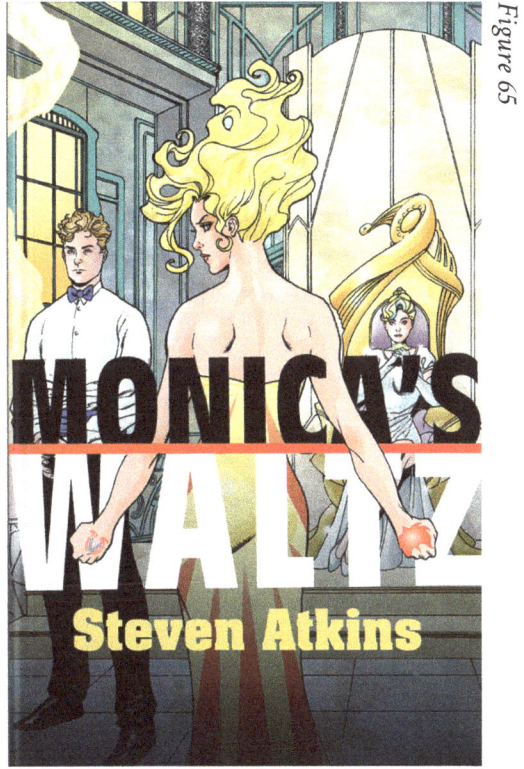

Figure 65

Figure 66

I sent them through to the author, feeling quite pleased with myself. They weren't covers I would have created had I the opportunity to select the imagery myself, but I definitely wasn't embarrassed by them. The author, in a nutshell, rejected them all. I'd altered his illustration too much. And he also hated my font choices. He had hired me to do a job that *he* wanted, and he was not open to negotiation or discussion. He did not care about sales. All he wanted was a book that *he* loved. So, I had an obligation.

Take a look at Figure 67 for what he wanted and walked away with.

Okay, it's not a "bad" cover, but it doesn't represent me as a designer, and I would not endorse this cover as a sample of something that would serve the book well in the marketplace. So, I decided that I preferred to leave my design credit off

77

Figure 67

this cover and I simply credited the illustrator, who was clearly talented in his field. What this author wanted from me was basically my technical ability, not my design experience. There are a couple of things to note about this.

1. *You, as the author, are ultimately the boss*, but are your personal preferences really going to give your book the best chances of survival in the market?

2. *The whole point in hiring a designer is to take advantage of their creative talent and skills.* If all you need is someone with computer and software skills, don't waste your money on hiring a professional book cover designer. Ask a friend for help. No suitable friends? Hire tech help. But please be very careful of people on Fivrr. (I once found multiple "designers" on there using *my* designs in their portfolio. Of course, I got them removed from the platform!)

I beg you, if you are about to approach a designer with an illustration that was not illustrated by someone with book cover design experience, please reconsider unless you will allow your designer to manipulate it.

Sometimes projects like *Monica's Waltz* hit my inbox. And sometimes I'll offer a hand, for a price, and sometimes I'll just end up turning them down. Because I'd rather spend my energy on projects that are also going to fulfill me creatively, not just make me money. And even though that should also be your goal, an open mind, and accepting that others might have better ideas than the ones you are married to for personal reasons, might help you achieve that. "Killing your darlings" doesn't only apply to writing!

So, I've managed to go off on a bit of a tangent, but I think it was a beneficial one because it shows how important it is to allow the designer to create the text and imagery at the same time.

To further show you how text and image synergy (or lack thereof) can make or break a cover, have a look at two examples of sample covers (Figures 68–73) that an assistant-in-training designed for me, and the same covers after my creative input. Please note that some of these covers still have watermarks in them, as they are pulled from my samples, in which I do not use the high-resolution images.

As you can see, my assistant had the ideas there, but when I, who had a little more experience, stepped in, I was able to give those covers that bit of creative flair that they needed to come alive.

I remember once giving a workshop on book cover design, using these examples, and one of the participants said in the chat window, "I hope Jessica's designs were the ones on the left. I liked those better." The other participants didn't agree with him, but it really does go to show that it's all about targeting the right audience. He was a sci-fi writer, and they were definitely not sci-fi books. The one thing that is going to really help sell your book is making sure to identify your audience before getting a cover designed.

Figure 68 Assistant's design

Figure 69 My revision

Figure 70 What it eventually became (used for another book)

Figure 71 Assistant's Design

Figure 72 My revision

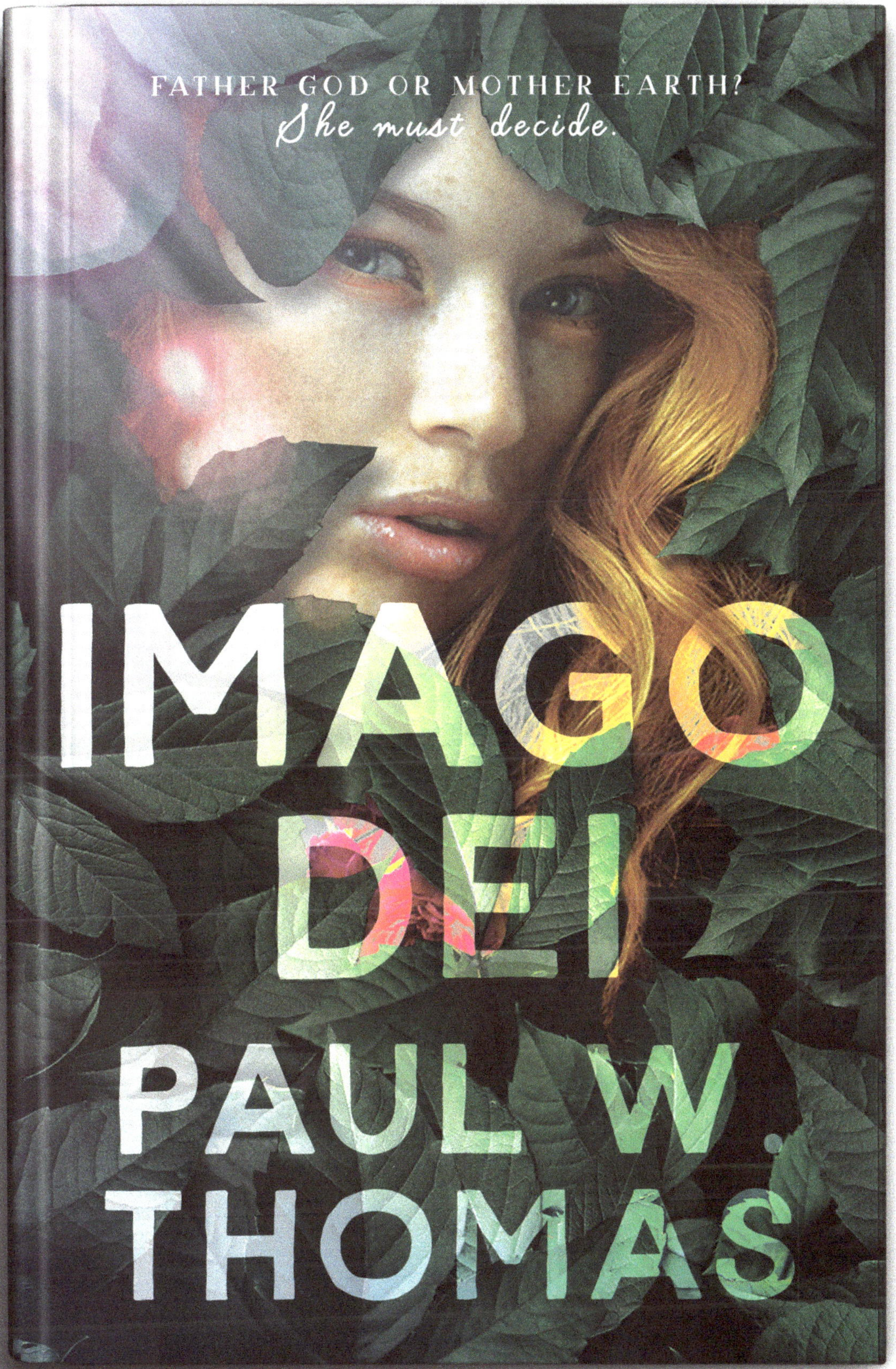

FATHER GOD OR MOTHER EARTH?
She must decide.

IMAGO DEI
PAUL W. THOMAS

Figure 73 What it eventually became

Working with an assistant

In order to keep up with booking demands, it was essential for me to hire an assistant. Especially after becoming a mother.

Just to give you an idea of how I collaborate with an assistant and how it affects my design work, I typically do most of the initial creative work (the three samples), and then hand over revisions, and other file formats for them to complete. But I also *do* hand over full projects if I think they can handle it, and if they are good with the genre.

My first assistant, Emily Reading, with whom I worked for three years, was extremely talented in creating historical, fantasy and sci-fi covers, but not so much with nonfiction, literary, contemporary and poetry. I had to learn that through trial and error, so in the beginning of our working relationship, I had to sometimes take over some projects to get them back on track, or offer extensive creative guidance for her to follow.

But there were also many covers that she absolutely nailed. She had ideas that I probably wouldn't have come up with myself, but worked so well. Take a look at Figures 74 and 75, which are a couple of hers that I was super impressed by.

Figure 74

JACKSON MCGARRY

RUNNING ON MAYBE

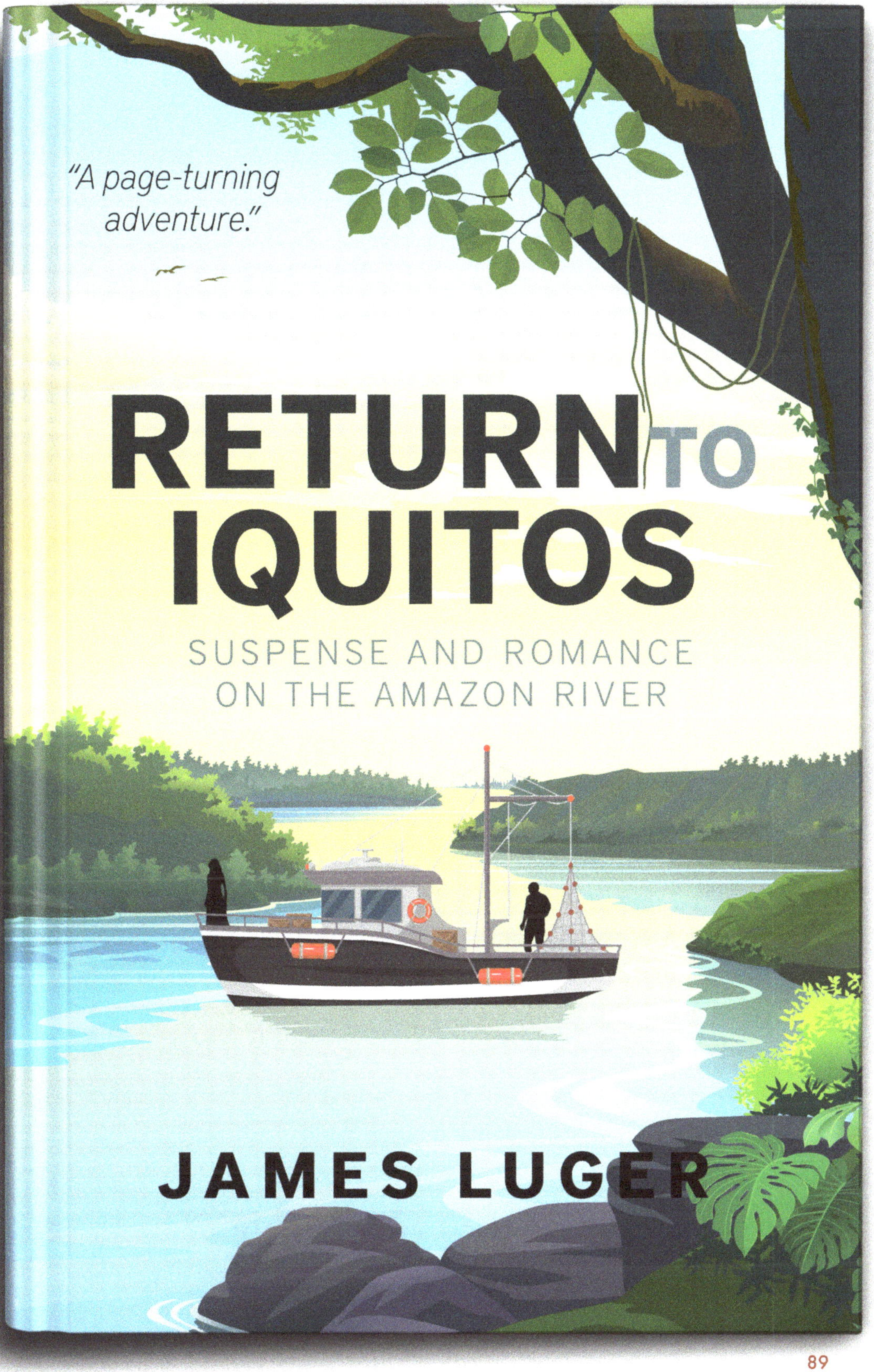

Figure 75

"A page-turning adventure."

RETURN TO IQUITOS

SUSPENSE AND ROMANCE ON THE AMAZON RIVER

JAMES LUGER

I was very sad to see her go, but thankfully she's still on social media duty. She's the one who posts all my socials posts with my book cover work. She also sells her own premade covers. If you want to check her out, go to *ereadingpublishing.com*. She does a lot of 3D rendering and combines it with her own photography.

After working with Emily, I learned a big lesson. I was expecting her to just pick up what I liked and be able to replicate my own creative style. You can't make someone replicate someone else's creative style. You need to find someone who already has it, or at least thinks similarly, so that you can mold their ideas. You can't mold ideas that are the complete opposite.

It wasn't her fault that she wasn't consistently giving me what I wanted. It was mine. From a business perspective, I shouldn't have just taken on the first designer I liked and assumed that things would just work. This is a great example of why you need to choose your designer wisely and carefully, which I will talk about in the next section.

I now have a new assistant with whom I've been working with for less than a month. So far, I haven't a single complaint. But I didn't have any complaints about Emily's work in the beginning either, so wish me luck!

I think this business, in general, is very hit and miss. And not only regarding assistants. You might see the most gorgeous cover you've ever seen, and then discover that the book doesn't sell very well. There are likely other factors at play then, like metadata issues, which I will touch upon a little later. But even if you do have all your ducks in a row, it doesn't mean your book is going to be a best-seller, so make sure you've got realistic expectations.

DIY author designs vs. makeovers from professionals

First up is a cover from Jean Gill who is an amazing photographer, and I have therefore used many of her photographs in her book covers. But being a brilliant photographer doesn't necessarily mean she's able to design a great book cover with them. And just to even the playing field here, I wouldn't be able to take such beautiful photographs either! We all have different skills, so don't sweat it if you are an illustrator, for example, who can't nail cover design. It's a very different beast. Figure 76 is Jean's original cover, and Figure 77 is mine. The photographs of the dogs and the mountains are hers.

Check out Jean Gill's books and photography here: *jeangill.com*.

Figure 76

Figure 77

Debbie Young didn't intend to use her DIY cover (Figure 78), she simply created it as a mock-up for her designer as an example of what she wanted. Thank goodness! Rachel Lawston's design (Figure 79) is absolutely brilliant.

Learn more about Debbie and Rachel here:
authordebbieyoung.com
lawstondesign.com

Figure 78   *Figure 79*

The following book went through a complete overhaul when it was picked it up by Vine Leaves Press. It was originally published elsewhere with a different title. It also underwent a development edit so the contents of the book were also revised. I'm not sure who designed the original cover (Figure 80, probably best I don't say anyway!), but I designed the remake (Figure 81).

Learn more about Tom Gillespie and Vine Leaves Press here:
tom-gillespie.com
vineleavespress.com

Figure 80

Figure 81

When I asked for DIY examples, Anne Renwick was very reluctant and embarrassed by her DIY cover (Figure 82), but I have to say, she didn't do too bad a job, did she? Her designer at Book Fly Design, certainly gave it some oomph (Figure 83), but the inspiration was clearly based on the original design, so kudos, Anne!

Learn more about Anne and Book Fly Design here:
annerenwick.com
bookflydesign.com

Figure 82

Figure 83

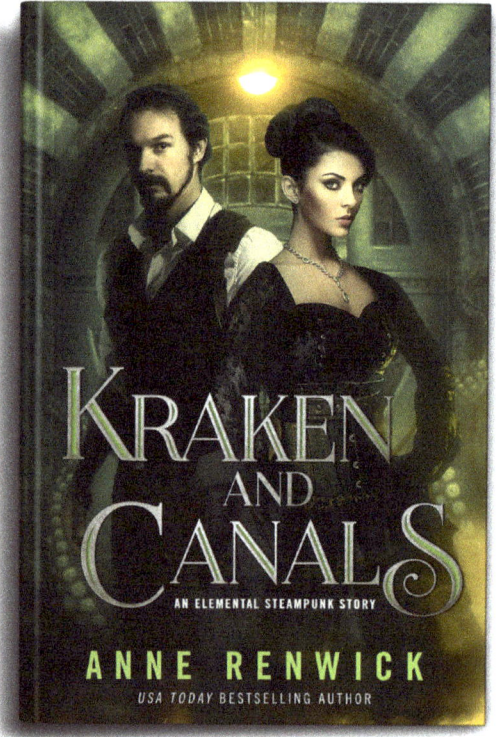

Researching and Choosing a Book Cover Designer

There are a lot of us around now. A simple internet search for "book cover designer" will bring up a plethora of options. But who to choose?

To start, take a look at some online lists from successful authors and publishing consultants that recommend the best of the best. I would start with the lists that you can currently find on Kindlepreneur, Makeuseof.com, The Creative Penn, and John Fox. A quick search online will bring those up. If you're a member of The Alliance of Independent Authors, you'll also find a list of vetted service providers in their Partner Directory, who may also offer discounts. For example, I offer 10% off to ALLi members. *Refer to Appendix G for the link.*

Countless times in my career I've heard authors complain that their cover designers have disappointed them. But this isn't always the designer's fault. If an author hasn't done their research properly, or they have rushed into a decision, then their choice of designer was not a wise one. You need to spend quality time looking at portfolios to make sure you like their style and that you would work well as partners. Because it *is* a partnership. If you are hiring a designer because they are cheap, that's the wrong reason. If you are hiring a designer because a friend recommended them, that's also the wrong reason. If you are hiring a designer because you are incredibly in love with their portfolio, then *that* is the right reason.

Here are some questions to ask yourself while doing your research.

1. *Have they designed covers in your genre?* Keep in mind that if you can't see your genre in their portfolio, it doesn't mean they can't do it. It may just be that they've selected the covers that they personally like, so if you like their style, it's best to ask directly.

2. *Are you attracted to their work?* Are there any examples that make you want to pick up the book and read the blurb?

3. *Are their examples competitive with covers of currently bestselling titles in your genre?* If you don't know, you should take a look on Amazon and in the country you believe you will sell the most because the bestselling books in the US vs. the UK, for example, are very different.

4. *Do their covers excite you?* Do you want to get in touch with the designer right this minute to inquire about availability?

5. *Is the price right for you?* If you can't afford them, please don't settle for a designer who you aren't sure about simply because they are cheaper. It's likely to end up a complete waste of your money, and you still won't end up with a cover you like. Save your pennies and hire the designer you want to work with when you have the money.

6. *Are you being offered a decent number of samples and revisions for the price, or will you have to pay extra for changes?* For around $500 to $700 USD, I believe you should at the very least receive an eBook cover delivered as a JPEG at 300 dpi and at the trim size dimensions; a paperback cover file in PDF delivered in accordance with the printer/distributor guidelines/specifications, which will always include the back, spine, and front as one image; a 3D mock-up of the book in PNG with a transparent background which can be used on your website or socials for publicity purposes; and two or three

stock images with standard license included, two or more sample designs, and three revisions.

7. *Read through their terms and conditions, and especially keep an eye out for mentions of copyright.* Some designers are happy to hand over source files and grant their clients full control over what they decide to do with them. Basically, they are handing over all the rights to their work. I am not one of those designers. You may think that's unfair since you are paying me to design something for *your* book, but let me explain myself.

I believe in intellectual property and my reputation as a designer. If I just handed over my design files without any rules attached, an author/publisher could potentially alter the design, ruin it, publish it, and still plaster over the internet that I designed it when it no longer looks like anything I would have ever delivered or be proud of showing in my portfolio.

These consequences would make it look like I designed sub-par covers and destroy my business. So, my prices are fair and reflect the time and expertise I put into the work. For that price, I allow my clients to unconditionally and perpetually use the files I deliver to them. This means the completed cover files that both the client and I are proud of releasing into the world. Fair? "Yes, but what if I want to make changes in the future?" you ask. I have two options for that: a) you come back to me to make changes that are going to be done properly at an hourly rate, or 2) you buy the source files and receive a binding license which you can check out in Appendix A.

8. *Who licenses the stock images and what kind of licenses do they get?* Be aware that the designer would be purchasing a "standard license" to any stock imagery that will be used in your design. Stock imagery that I use is usually manipulated so much that it's unrecognizable,

but if your designer has found the perfect image, and hasn't altered it at all, it's probably safer for you to obtain those licenses too. It's a pretty furry subject, and some people have a lot of opinions about the legal use of stock, so you might want to do a bit of reading on the subject. Also note that there are rules we need to follow regarding the use of the stock images themselves, and there are different kinds of licenses you can buy with various restrictions attached. Here are the basics copied verbatim from Adobe stock images about the Standard License:

> With a Standard license, you may:
>
> - Reproduce up to 500,000 copies of the asset in all media, including product packaging, printed marketing materials, digital documents, or software.
> - Include the asset in email marketing, mobile advertising, or a broadcast or digital program if the expected number of viewers is fewer than 500,000.
> - Post the asset to a website or social media site with no limitation on views.
> - Include the asset in some types of products, such as inside a textbook, as long as the primary value of the product is not the asset itself, and the product is not reproduced more than 500,000 times.
> - Share the unmodified asset with your employees and contractors who have contractually agreed to abide by the license terms.
> - Transfer the license to your client or employer.
>
> With a Standard license, you may not:
>
> - Distribute the stand-alone file.
> - Create merchandise, templates, or other products for resale or distribution where the primary value of the product is associated with the asset itself. For example, you can't use the asset to create a poster, t-shirt, or coffee mug that someone would buy specifically because of the asset printed on it.
> - Transfer the license to more than one employer or client, unless separately licensed for each.

In a nutshell, purchasing a standard license will be enough for your needs. If you happen to sell over 500,000 copies of your book, you can then afford to upgrade to the Enhanced License. See the types of licenses available here: *stock.adobe.com/license-terms.*

Avoid, however, editorial images. One, they cost an arm and a leg, and a brain. Two, they can only be used by people such as journalists, and cannot be altered in any way, artistically or otherwise. They have to be published exactly as they are. Yes, the wording on the licenses can be a little confusing, and yes, I promise, using stock with a standard license for your book is legal, so please stop worrying.

9. *Does the designer kick off the deal with a project agreement/contract that you have to both sign?* If yes, good, you can trust them. If not, it's not the end of the world, but make sure you have everything they promise to deliver, and timelines locked down, in writing before handing over any money should something go sideways. There is no standard contract we use, but you can see mine as an example in Appendix B.

10. *Do they require an upfront payment? If so, how much and are you happy with that?* I require 50% upfront, non-refundable, and the remaining 50% once final files are delivered. Don't think that's fair? I'll tell you why it is. If I didn't require a non-refundable deposit, I could potentially fill my schedule with projects from clients who aren't serious about committing. I can't afford to fill up my calendar with non-paying projects, and then end up turning away serious clients because I think I can't fit them in. I would then be left with, let's say, a month of no work and no money when they don't show up. If your designer requires upfront payment in full before beginning work, I would totally question that if it isn't at least partially refundable.

11. *How quickly did they respond to your enquiry? Did their response sound friendly, cold, vague, confusing, blunt, or over-detailed?* None of these are necessarily wrong, or bad, but certain personalities may clash and that may lead to misunderstandings and disagreements. If you react in a negative way to their response, my advice is to move on. The way they make you feel now is going to determine how well you get along as collaborators. Because this *is* a collaboration. You need each other equally to make this work. And you need to be able to communicate well. The same goes for the designer, so when you send them an inquiry, try to give them the same respect and treatment you expect in return. Remember, everyone is human behind the screen … except, maybe, Amazon customer service. :-)

Client: You can see the original cover on my Amazon page, which you'll find easily if you spell my name correctly.

Me thinking: Thank you for assuming I'm stupid.

SOME OF THE BIGGEST CHALLENGES AN AUTHOR AND A DESIGNER FACE DURING A COLLABORATION

Me: What genre is it?

Client: Each novel has multiple POVs; 3rd person past tense. The novellas are limited 3rd person, past tense and feature a female secondary character.

Me thinking: That is not what I asked.

1. *When a client doesn't know what they want, or understand the basics of what is needed.*

Some clients come to me not knowing, even the tiniest bit, what they want their book cover to look like. This coupled with an author not understanding which genre their book falls under can be a disaster. But occasionally, it can be a blessing.

I have to be honest. I love being given free creative rein, and trusted to do right by the author and the book. I do my best work when I'm allowed to take creative control. *But,* it can be a bit dangerous. Occasionally, an author won't like what I've designed. And rather than telling me what they *do* like, they tell me everything they *don't* like. This is incredibly unhelpful because ruling out dislikes, without stating likes as well, means the possibilities of likes are pretty much endless, and I can't create endless design samples until I hit the jackpot for the price of three.

This scenario can typically happen when a client's questionnaire answers do not truly represent the book. And dodgy answers usually mean the author hasn't got a firm grasp yet on what their book is about. Sometimes after authors have read through my questionnaire (Appendix C), they come back saying that it made them realize that their manuscript wasn't ready, and that they would like to make more revisions before moving forward with a cover. Kudos.

2. *When a client is married to ideas that will not work.*

There are various reasons why an idea may not work, so let me go through a couple of them with you.

The biggest reason I encounter is that there is no stock available to bring an idea into fruition. Stock imagery is fantastic, but it's not without limitations. Though I do combine multiple images and manipulate them to create a completely unique piece of cover art, sometimes specific details cannot be achieved. This is why an idea needs to be broad and general when working with stock, so that I have wiggle room to create something "like" it.

For example, I cannot do this:

It was like she was three pieces of toast leaning together wearing an ornate dress. Massive jewels dangled from everywhere. Mrs. Toast had snakes for arms and her head was a box suspended by a ridiculously thin neck. Legs were replaced by stumpy-looking snakes minus heads.

Yes, this was a real request! I said, "sorry mate, not happenin'" (Not in those words.)

You need to remember that not all graphic designers are illustrators too. If you are after an illustrator, make sure you're clear about that in your inquiry. Illustration is also a lot more expensive than graphic design using stock, and not every illustrator is experienced with book cover design. If you're after a heavily customized illustrated cover, sometimes the best way forward is for an illustrator and a book cover designer to collaborate on your project together.

Here is a description of something I *can* do:

Muted colors and handwriting (using a postcard supplied by me). Although many of the postcards have been treasured and are in excellent condition, a few creases that convey the passing of time would suggest age and I'm actually keen to have some tatty edges. I like the idea of having some of my postcards arranged with the handwriting on show. Then as the main image, one or two of my postcards overlapping. All of the reverse sides of the cards I have selected for you have green stamps – perhaps pick out that in some way? It's important that the cover shows both sides of the cards – the messages are what the book's about, not the images.

Have a look at Figure 84 for the result.

A second reason why an idea may not work is when it will not look good on, or as, a book cover. Sometimes an author will ask me to do something that may look gorgeous as an art piece in a gallery, for example, or in a comic book, like the cover for *Monica's Waltz* I showed you, but leaves a lot to be desired on a book cover. As I mentioned earlier, the image and text needs to be designed simultaneously for them to work well together. When an artist creates a painting, or an illustrator an illustration, space for text has not

Figure 84

been taken into consideration. Similarly, there may not be any free space at all in the piece, or there may be too many colors, details, elements, that confuse the eye. The beauty of a painting is that you can look at it on a wall for hours and consistently find new things to admire, new metaphors to decipher, and symbolism to analyze. A book cover has an immediate impact, and typically that impact doesn't change over time, which is exactly what you need from a book cover.

I will always try to explain to clients why it doesn't look good, and most of the time I am successful in convincing them and I avoid having to create something that I'm embarrassed by. But sometimes I will encounter a stubborn client who insists I do exactly what they want regardless of my opinion. In this case, I grit my teeth and do what they want, and leave my design credit off the cover. Never mind. I can't win them all.

Something also to note, that is vaguely related, is the issue of a client loving all my samples, choosing one with great excitement, and then asking for revisions that make it unrecognizable. I have one thing to say about that: *Don't fix somethin' that ain't broke.*

Me: Can you please be more specific re your comment *It needs a few changes?*

Client: Yeah, I think the sky needs more layers.

Me: More layers of what? Clouds?

Client: No, sky.

THE BALANCE BETWEEN CREATING A BOOK COVER THE AUTHOR LOVES, THE DESIGNER LOVES, AND A POTENTIAL READER LOVES

Author vs. Reader

As writers, we've all heard the advice, "write what you know." I don't interpret this as writing about experiences that we've had first-hand, but as subject matter we feel passionate enough to write about. If we don't write from the heart, from a place of honesty, then it's unlikely readers will get emotionally invested in our work.

In the over ten years I've been doing this job, eighty percent of my clients come to me with cover art ideas loaded with personal meaning that does not translate well when designed. Unfortunately, when it comes to covers, an author who isn't experienced in book cover design, or isn't willing to learn, needs to let go of those ideas to end up with a competitive cover. When a reader sees a cover, they aren't likely to relate to it in the same way the author of the book does because they haven't read the book yet.

Just for a moment, put yourself into the shoes of a reader browsing through a physical bookstore. What thoughts go through your head when you are inclined to pick up a book and read the back cover? For me, as a fan of literary and speculative fiction, memoir and mind, body, spirit nonfiction (I love books about the brain!), it's something like the following:

FICTION
… oh, this reminds me of …
… oh, this looks like a good character-driven read for a rainy day …
… hmm, this might be too soppy. I want a bit of grit. Pass …
… ooh, this looks like something I could enjoy over summer …

NONFICTION
… oh, this looks like an entertaining take on the subject …
… hmm, too authoritative and bland. I want sassy! …
… oh, that looks like advice I could benefit from …
… hmm, I don't think I could take this author seriously …

What are my thoughts *dripping* with? *Expectation.*

So how do we strike a balance between meeting a reader's expectations and fulfilling an author's expectations? As an author, try to keep an open mind, and understand that your book cover designer knows what they are doing and what readers want. A designer doesn't only want to create something beautiful for a bookshelf, they want to create something that functions. And that function is to entice and sell.

I understand, as a writer, marketing is a secondary consideration. When I started out as an author, I thought that I'd just be able to hire someone else to do it, and forget about it. You *can* hire someone else to do it, but you can't forget about it. One of the greatest pieces of advice I can offer you as an author regarding marketing is: don't fight it if you don't understand it. Your desires will never just be disregarded. If there is any way to use them *and* please your audience, it will be done!

Jessica Bell

Designer vs. Author

Many authors forget that designers aren't *just* service for hire. We are also creators of art. That means we are investing our creative souls into an author's project too. I can't speak for other designers, but if I didn't let myself get creatively and emotionally invested in my work, it wouldn't be worth publishing. This means that there is a fine line between satisfying my artist's soul and delivering a cover that the author is in love with too. Don't get me wrong, if I give myself credit as the designer, it means that I love the cover too, and that I'm proud to display it as part of my portfolio. But sometimes there are covers that make my heart sing so much that I can't believe I was the one who actually created them. I'm sure, as writers, you can relate to this feeling. I experience this with my own writing and song writing sometimes too.

Since I always create three sample designs to begin with, it is always with great suspense when I send them through to the client. Though I'm always happy with them all, there is typically one sample that is my "baby"; the sample that is the wild card; the sample which I decided to go out on a limb and deviate from the brief a little. When I design these wild cards, I design them from the perspective of my Vine Leaves Press publisher hat who has total creative control over the cover design of VLP books. When designing for VLP I always try to do something a little different while also attracting the intended audience. With fingers crossed, I hit send. Sometimes the client chooses my baby, and sometimes they don't. If the latter happens, I of course have a little internal cry, but then get on with the job. Luckily, I am set up to sell my babies as pre-made covers for a fraction of the typical cost.

Designer vs. Reader

Sometimes when I'm browsing through Amazon bestsellers, looking through covers for inspiration, I feel a great sense of loss. This is because I'm constantly faced with the same formulas over and over. And I'm bored. Take a look at all the orange covers of books set in Africa in Figure 85 when I searched the internet for "books set in Africa."

I'm bored of all the orange covers of novels set in Africa. I'm bored of all the thriller covers with shadowy figures walking into the distance. I'm bored of all the beach reads set in Greece with women clutching their sunhats looking off into the horizon. I could go on. But I won't. I won't because rather than this having a negative impact on me, it has a positive one. I want to challenge myself to use these trendy tropes and make them even more attractive and beautiful and unique. I will not settle for "that looks about right." My aim is to get readers to adore the cover as much as the book, and hopefully enhance their reading experience.

Figure 85

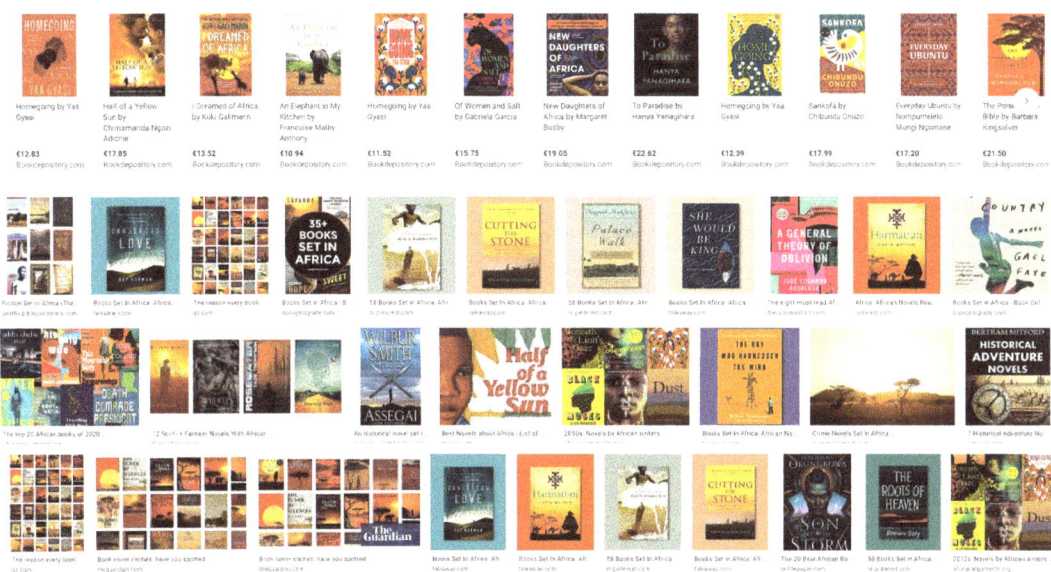

HOW TO PREPARE FOR A COLLABORATION

Me: Describe the appearance of your protagonist.

Client: Good looking in a nondescript way.

Me: Describe the setting.

Client: The town itself has a population of about three hundred thousand.

Me: [Sigh]

Are you really *really* ready for a cover designer? If you've never self-published before, you might be surprised to realize that you still have a lot to prepare before having your designer begin work.

Let's first begin with the technical details that around 50% of my author clients forget they need to know.

Me: **Please copy/paste all your cover copy here (e.g. title, author name, back cover blurb, puff quotes, publisher URLs, plus any other information you'd like to include).**

Client: **Sorry. Not sure I have these. Do you mean from older published works?**

Let's talk about your …

Front cover copy

Title

First up is your title. Yes, you need one before a designer begins work. And it needs to be one hundred percent locked in. Changing a title after the cover is designed is one of my biggest nightmares, hence the title of this book! The length of it, the shape of the letters, the positioning of the words, are all considered when designing a cover. Even changing a word from singular to plural could potentially mess up the design. I'm not kidding. Take a look at Figure 86 (and the cover of *this* book!), and think about how adding or subtracting words to/from the title would affect the design.

Figure 86

Author name

You need to supply the name that you want visible on the front cover. If you want to use a pseudonym, and haven't decided on it yet, now is the time to do so for reasons described above.

Puff quote

A puff quote is an endorsement for your book that has been provided by another author, professional in your field, or a publication that published book reviews.

Example:

"Extraordinary, chilling, and unique."
Jessica Bell, award-winning author of *GO*

In order to obtain one, you will have had to send out advanced copies to readers/reviewers. Advanced reviews (aka puff quotes) can come from fellow authors, publishing professionals, and/or colleagues or literary professionals, such as a writing professor, as well. If you are writing nonfiction, you can also approach others in your field who are not writers. For example, if you are writing about child psychology, approach a fellow child psychologist. If you are writing about your experience in the war, approach another veteran.

Typically, individual readers need around one month to deliver. If it's out for editorial review, mainstream media typically require three (and sometimes even four) months' lead time.

For more information about puff quotes, check out Appendix D.

By the way, I didn't have enough time to get one for the cover of this book, as you'll have noticed, so I left a placeholder there... JOKE!

Tag line

A tag line is like an elevator pitch for your book.

Example:

They kidnapped the wrong girl.

Unless your cover design is generous on space, I advise you don't include both a tag line and a puff quote on the cover. It's not unusual to include both, but depending on the design and genre, it just might not look any good. Take a look at Figure 87 as an example of a cover where both of them do work.

> *Me:* What do you envision your cover to look like?

> *Client:* I envision the title, subtitle, and my by-line on a photo.

> *Me:* Hmm …

Figure 87

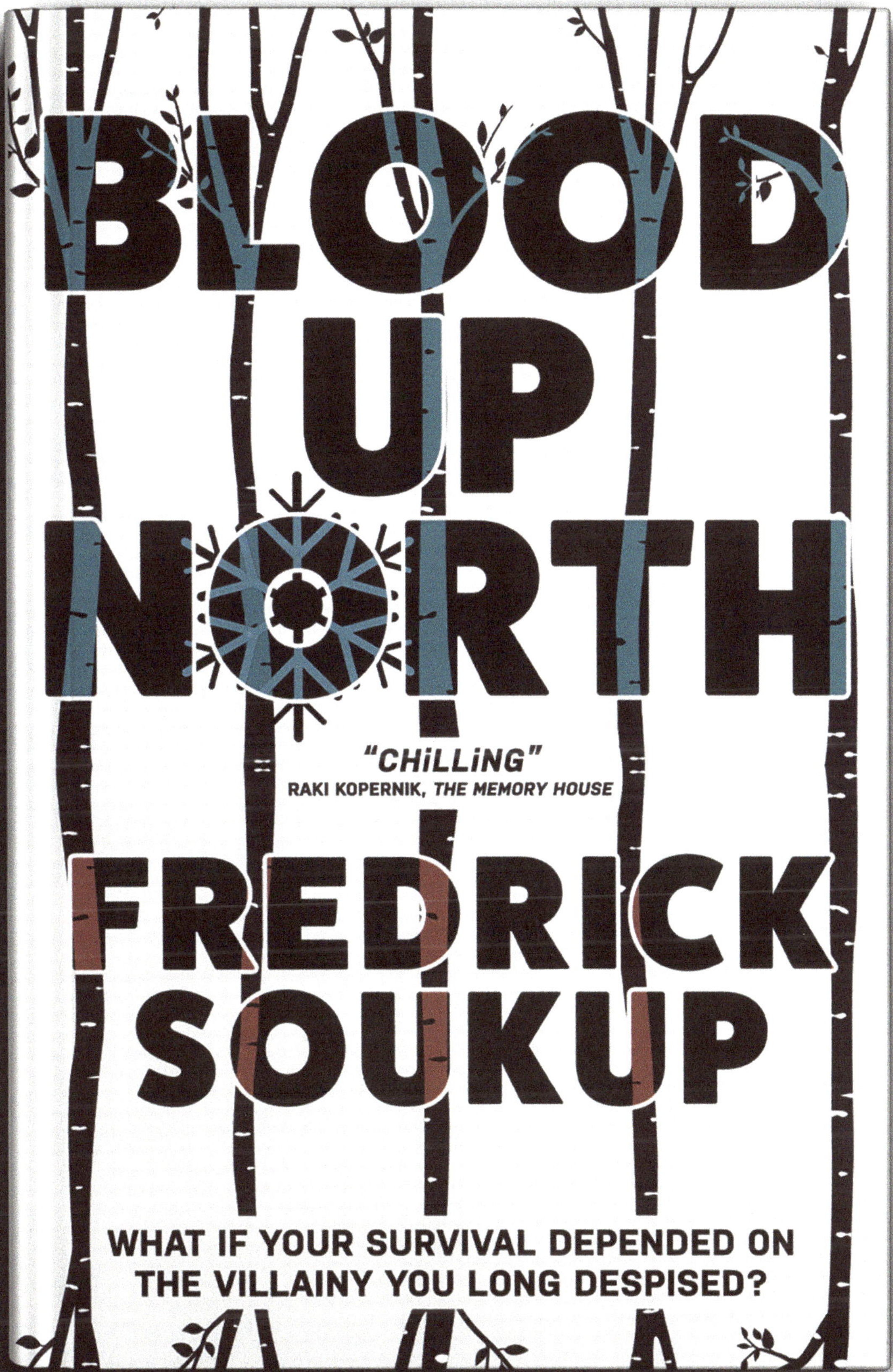

BLOOD UP NORTH

"CHiLLiNG"
RAKI KOPERNIK, *THE MEMORY HOUSE*

FREDRICK SOUKUP

WHAT IF YOUR SURVIVAL DEPENDED ON THE VILLAINY YOU LONG DESPISED?

Back cover copy

Book description (aka blurb or jacket copy)

I know they are hard to write, but please don't do this…

"Jessica, let's just leave the back cover blank. It will give it an air of mystery."

Don't be lazy. What will you put on Amazon? If you can't write it yourself, ask someone for help.

Try reading six or eight blurbs from books in the same genre on your shelf or eReader to get a feeling for pace, tone, and the kinds of details authors include before writing a draft. Then, show that draft to a fellow writer; friends often offer feedback of this kind for free or the price of a coffee and a good conversation.

People who will offer quality help writing a blurb might include a friend from book club who has likely read a lot of back cover copy, a best friend who reads a lot, or a writing group leader—all of whom would likely offer help for free or nearly free (buying that person a gift-card or giving them a free copy of the book later is a nice courtesy, if they do offer help without payment). People to avoid asking for blurb help? Significant others, friends who haven't read a book this year or in a few years, friends who don't read the same genre as the book, and co-workers.

You could also hire a freelance author and/or editor or copy writer. Many creative writing teachers who freelance love getting short-term freelance assignments from authors who aren't sure how to write a blurb; it provides another writing professional with some income and goodwill, and it can sometimes be easier for someone who hasn't written the book to pull out the essential information that will appeal most to readers without getting bogged down in specific details. Also, it's eye-opening and fun to hear what another writer finds most essential about your book in their description.

There are also grad students and university students majoring in English who would be happy to get a short-term gig like this, sometimes in exchange for a recommendation or endorsement for their website.

And don't worry, you can still edit the book description after it's been placed on the back cover. The space it will have *is* dependent on the design, but it's never as intricate a process as it is for the front cover. But you *do* need to provide something. If not initially for the back cover, for the designer's broad understanding of what the book is about.

I know, as authors, we often have a message, and explore various themes, and sometimes we want readers to *learn* from our fiction. But please try and refrain from focusing on those aspects in your blurb. Readers do not want to learn; they want a story to sink their teeth into. Story, conflict, action … not a book report.

Here is a sample *don't* and a *do*. Thank you to Ann S. Epstein for allowing me to use her "book report" as an example!

> **DONT**
> *One Person's Loss* asks whether the marriage of young German Jewish refugees can survive their personal clashes and the traumas of the Holocaust. Set in Brooklyn from 1937 to 1951, Petra and Erich Wedler's parents send them to America to start a family before the Nazis systematically decimate their community. The novel is told from both perspectives, as

husband and wife find themselves at odds over losses—a miscarriage, the slaughter of loved ones—yet repeatedly reunited by love and hope. Can obsessive-compulsive Petra loosen her meticulous standards? Can careless Erich accept more responsibility for his actions? As the pair confront birth and death, their relationship seesaws until a final crisis tests their ability to sustain a balance.

The novel's emotional depth transcends its era. The family's challenges parallel those faced by today's migrants and refugees who are buffeted by violence, discrimination, and forces beyond their control and human understanding. The narrative measures the lengths to which parents will go to assure their children's safety and happiness, and questions the obligations adult children have toward parents who sacrificed for their well-being. Like life, the book is filled with sorrow, yet also relieved by periods of peace and leavened with moments of joy.

DO

It's 1937. Jewish newlyweds flee Nazi Germany for Brooklyn, admonished by their parents to have children to "save our people." Following a miscarriage, Petra becomes obsessed with adopting a Jewish infant abandoned at a Coney Island exhibit of incubator babies. Erich isn't so sure. A struggle begins about when—and even if—they should start a family.

Meanwhile, the couple agonizes over the fate of the families they left behind in Hitler's Europe. Can Petra's parents bribe officials and secure safe passage to the US? What of Erich's parents and four siblings, especially his hot-headed brother who joined the resistance?

One Person's Loss explores whether marriage, even grounded in love, can survive personal clashes and the traumas of the Holocaust.

Client: Here's the text for the back cover. I assume you do the background image, too? Would like to see it before we go to press, if possible.

Me: Yes, of course you'll see the cover before it goes to press. I don't send the cover to press, I send it to you, and then you send to press.

ISBN

Your designer also needs your ISBN for all commissioned physical formats. Please do not buy barcodes. Your designer will be able to generate those for you for free as long as you provide them with the ISBNs. If you're distributing via Amazon's KDP, please don't let them just slap on their own barcode in the bottom right-hand corner. It's ugly. Let your designer create a professional-looking barcode area that includes your logo.

For information about obtaining ISBNs refer to Appendix E.

Author/publisher website and logo

These will be included in your barcode area and the logo will also go on the spine.

Figure 88

Have a look at the full dust jacket of *Small Forgotten Moments* (Figure 88) by Annalisa Crawford for an example of how everything is laid out. Note that this book doesn't have a typical spine. For a typical spine refer to Figure 32 or 60.

If you don't have a logo, ask your designer to make one. The cost for a logo can vary, depending on your brief. For example, if you intend to become a fully-fledged publisher, you'll need to discuss your goals, motivations, and the story of who you are as a business, which will lead to brainstorming marketing strategy in order to create a logo with deeper meaning. That's going to cost a lot more than you saying, "hey, just whip something up for me using the first letters of my name so my book looks professional." Sometimes I will do the latter for free with the cover design if the author doesn't want to bother with it. But if you want to go the full hog, be sure to mention that in your inquiry.

If you don't have a website, also get one. In this day and age, it's essential.

Also, I advise you keep the book price off the barcode. It will make life easy for you if you ever decide to change it. If you do include it, you will have to get your designer to revise the files for you and you'll have to reupload them to your distributor, which can also cost you money.

Me: What is your URL?

Client: [quotes me ISBN]

Distributor/printer and tech specifications

1. Distributor/printer

Your designer needs to know who you are printing/distributing with, since every company has different file submission guidelines. As an independent author, the most popular choices of book distributor for eBook and paperback, which also double as printers, are Kindle Direct Publishing, IngramSpark, and PublishDrive. For a larger list of distribution services, you should check out the ALLi Self-Publishing Services Directory. If you are using a local printer, rather than a Print-on-Demand company, you'll need to source their file submission specs and pass them along to your designer. Don't forget that if you're planning to print in bulk and warehouse your books, you will also need to select a separate distributor. In this case, however, your designer only needs to obtain the specs from your printer.

2. Trim size

This refers to the physical dimensions of your closed book. E.g., 5 x 8 inches (12.7 x 20.32 cm.) Have a look at Figure 89 for the most common trim sizes for a novel.

You may feel that you needn't decide on this right away, but you do. If your designer creates a cover to the incorrect dimensions, it may not be so simple to change and it may incur extra cost. Based on the trim size, we allocate a certain area of the imagery to expand over the margins. This is called a bleed. And if that amount is exact, and then you decide your trim size needs to be bigger, it's going to

Figure 89

take time to manipulate the image to extend it, or to rearrange the design to fit. So be sure about the trim size you choose. But when you choose, be sure to refer to the websites of your chosen distribution/printing partner to make sure they have those sizes, since not all Print-on-Demand services offer them all.

For an extensive list of sizes, please refer to Appendix F.

Me: What's the trim size of your book?

Client: Presently 0" x 0"

This cracked me up!

3. Page count

The final locked-in page count of your typeset book is needed in order to produce the cover files for all physical formats. This is because the page count determines the spine width. Most of my clients don't have this ready when they approach me, but that's okay. Most designers will be happy to design the front (eBook cover) and then proceed with the paperback/hardcover once the typeset pages are completed. Some designers (me included) also offer typesetting and eBook formatting services, so if you don't have that lined up, just ask.

Me: What's your page count?

Client: Jessica, the actual text of the book will be approximately 270 pages; additionally the front includes the following pages: *Title; *Dedication; *Acknowledgement AND the back includes the following pages; *About the Author; and *a blank page.

Me: What's your total page count? I'm really bad at math. ;-)

4. Paper and binding options

This seems like a silly request, doesn't it? Well, it's totally not. This is because the different colors and types of paper available are all different thicknesses, and this also affects spine width. In Figure 90 you'll see the three paper colors available at IngramSpark. Top is white, middle is crème, and bottom is groundwood. Strangely, groundwood, despite being so much lighter than white and crème, is actually thicker.

The two leaders of POD (KDP and IngramSpark) offer most of the following options. KDP's options are rather limited, so be sure what you choose is available there if you are using them. Some of the

Figure 90

below are only available using offset printing. For easy reference, I have coded them as follows: KDP (Kindle Direct Publishing), ING (IngramSpark and Lightning Source), OFF (Offset). Offset means printing that requires plates to be made, i.e. it's what traditional publishers use if they intend to print very large quantities. The larger the number of books that you print with offset, the cheaper each book becomes to produce.

Paper options

Groundwood: 38lb/56gsm, looks and feels like the paper used in traditional mass market paperbacks. Very light and pleasant to hold. Will save dollars on shipping due to the light weight. Not advised for textbooks, or reference books, which are likely to be scribbled in, since the paper is porous and likely to wear and tear with repeated use. (ING, OFF)

Crème: 50lb/74gsm, slightly thicker than groundwood, but higher quality. Perfect for books under 200 pages. I would advise you avoid using this for very long novels. Definitely nothing over 300 pages as it will feel like holding a brick. However, if you're printing with KDP, it's really your only option, since they don't offer anything lighter. (KDP, ING, OFF)

White: 50lb/74gsm, same as crème, just not crème. Decent for color printing children's books and some nonfiction or reference books. Note, however, that this paper isn't gloss. (KDP, ING, OFF)

White: 70lb/104gsm, used for standard or premium color printing (like this one!) Great for photography books or graphic novels. This paper isn't gloss either. (ING, OFF)

Photo quality gloss: Printers that offer paper of this type, such as *Blurb.com*, have a wide variety of choices. It's impossible to list them all here, so do your research on their website. (OFF)

Note: This paper list is not extensive. These are just the most common choices, and what's widely available via POD. If you are planning to print in bulk and warehouse your books, ask your printer what paper choices they have available.

Binding options (paperback)

Perfect bound: paper glued to spine, gloss or matte finish. (KDP, ING, OFF)

Duplex perfect bound: (like this one!) paper glued to spine, gloss or matte finish, color printing on inner front and back covers. (ING, OFF)

Saddle stitch: for shorter books, folded spine, stitched together with thread, gloss or matte finish. (OFF)

Spiral bound: no spine, pages and cover joined together with a plastic or metallic spiral, gloss or matte finish. (OFF)

Binding options (hardcover)

Case laminate: pages glued to hardcover at ends, cover art glued to the cover, gloss or matte finish. (KDP, ING, OFF)

Jacketed case laminate: same as above plus a removable gloss or matte dust jacket. Can also choose to keep laminate blank under the jacket. (ING, OFF)

Cloth (blue or gray only at Ingram) + dust jacket: Textured feel, cloth-like finish, with or without gloss or matte jacket. (ING, OFF)

Spiral bound is also available for hardcover books in some places. (OFF)

Note: Dust jacket designs also include flaps that fold over the front and back covers, so be sure you take advantage of that space in your cover design. You could add reviews, author bio, author note, anything that is relevant to you and your book.

For a bigger list of binding options with diagrams, refer to Appendix H.

5. Cover finish

The POD choices are gloss or matte. The simple reason why this info is requested is because when creating the cover templates from

KDP and IngramSpark, this information is a required input and seems to be embedded into the template's metadata. (Metadata is backend information that isn't seen, just like the keywords and book categories you input into Amazon and other distributors so that people can find your book.) So, which do you choose? It's really a personal preference, but matte is generally preferred for novels and creative nonfiction and memoir, and gloss is generally preferred for textbooks, children's books, and other types of nonfiction, but honestly, these are stereotypes, so just choose the finish you personally prefer. I know that I prefer matte, and many people I know love the velvety texture of it, but I have also met people who touch my books and wince. If you're that kind of person, choose gloss.

It's best, however, to order proof copies so you can see and feel for yourself. Ingram charges $25 USD or equivalent for a proof copy (shipping included). Amazon charges print cost plus shipping. I personally never use the proof copy service. I just make sure my book is up for preorder three months in advance, and then purchase a real copy of the book, which ends up being cheaper. If there are errors, you have three months to upload revised files. You might also like to purchase two or three copies and have a couple of trustworthy advanced readers use that copy for reviewing purposes, and ask them to let you know if they spot any typos.

If you're not taking the POD route, your printer is likely to have other options you can choose. For example, foils, or embossing and Spot UV. More about those in the next section.

Fancy features

The following features are not available with POD printing, so if you want to use any of these, you'll have to find an offset printer. There are many out there, but one commonly used in the United Kingdom is Clays, and in the United States is IPG. If you want to go even bigger, check out Ingram or Baker & Taylor. Or you can find a local printer and distribute the books yourself. But that's a lot of work!

For links and a few more suggestions refer to Appendix G.

There are quite a few to choose from, and it's just a matter of personal preference and if the cover design/book interior lends itself well to certain features, so don't worry about whether you should or shouldn't use these. Go with your gut.

1. Embossing and debossing

Embossing gives your cover a raised texture that you can see and feel. It is created by pressing the paper from underneath, giving it a 3D effect. This cannot be done on hardcovers, but it can on hardcover dust jackets. Debossing is the opposite way around. The design is imprinted, causing depressions in the paper. This can be done on hardcovers. Have a look at Figure 91 for an example.

2. Foil stamping

This is the process of pressing hot metal foil into the cover of a book using a stamp. This can be done on both paperbacks and hardcovers. This can also be embossed/debossed for added effect. Have a look at Figure 92 for an example.

Figure 91

Figure 92

3. Slip case

This is a robust presentation box which can also be used for a special edition, or with a collection or series of books. The "real" boxed set. Have a look at Figure 92 for an example.

4. Leather binding

Leather binding is costly, but if you want to create a special edition that resembles an old classic, this a beautiful and special option. Most leather-bound books utilize foil stamping and debossing to create a design on the cover. Have a look at Figure 93 for an example.

5. Gilded page edges

This is the process of applying a metallic foil to the outer edges of the book pages. It's typically done in gold and silver, but can actually be done in any color and doesn't need to be metallic. Have a look at Figure 93 for an example. I once read a gothic themed novel which had pages gilded in matte black. It looked like it had been dipped in charcoal dust. It was a very interesting look and attracted me to the book.

6. French flaps (aka French fold and gate fold covers)

These are book covers that are designed with a section that folds in on itself. It's one with the cover and cannot be removed. Just like on a dust jacket, you can add extra information on these flaps. Have a look at Figure 94 for an example.

Figure 93

Figure 94

7. Glossy inserts (aka plates)

Ever read a memoir with some glossy pages in the middle of the book full of photographs? Nice touch, but impossible with POD. Have a look at Figure 95 for an example.

8. Printed or colored endpapers

Endpapers are the end sheets of a book which sandwich the book block. It's a double-size folded sheet, one half pasted to the inner cover and the other side serving as the fly leaf. Have a look at Figure 96 for an example.

9. Spot UV

This is an application of a clear coating used to highlight specific areas of a cover. This can also be embossed/debossed for added effect. Have a look at Figure 97 for an example.

10. Ribbon marker

A narrow strip of fabric, often made of silk that is attached to the head of the spine to use as a bookmark. Have a look at Figure 98 for an example.

Note: This is by no means an extensive list. Ask what options your book printer has. Sometimes printers will have these things on their website, and sometimes not, so if you can't see something you want, email an inquiry. There might also be other options that attract you, especially if they do some handmade products.

Figure 95

Figure 96

Figure 97

Figure 98

HOW TO ENSURE A SMOOTH SAILING COLLABORATION

This section is written from the perspective of how I run my own design business and how my own creative mind works. I believe, from speaking to other book designers, that they have very similar processes and standards, but I cannot claim to be the representative voice for all of us. So please, don't forget to do your research to avoid collaborating with someone you might feel uncomfortable with.

Book a designer well in advance

I am typically booked out two months in advance, sometimes three, and I know for a fact that other popular designers are too. Most times when I get a request to begin a cover as soon as I am emailed, that author ends up having to look elsewhere. It's impossible for me to shove other projects aside. If you're lucky, you may catch me in the middle of a project that ended up finishing a lot more quickly than expected and I can therefore slot you in. But don't count on it.

Client: Invoice shows a Unit price of 200.00 Euros

Net Total = 170 Euros

Discount = 30 Euros

Total Due = 170.00 Euros

Does the Total Due reflect the 30 Euros Discount?

Will the designer read the entire manuscript?

No. There are a few reasons listed here in no order of importance.

Time.

My assistant and I can easily be juggling correspondence and actual design work of twenty different projects at a time. If we read every book before beginning work, we would not have roofs over our heads, or food in our bellies. Our kids would be sitting in the playground with empty lunch boxes, getting bullied … okay, I'll stop there. You get my drift.

Too much information.

Do you really want us to read your entire book and then face the same issues as you of not being able to decide what elements to use for inspiration? Remember, too many cooks always spoil the broth. And that includes ideas as well as people. Too many ideas result in indecisiveness. It also results in struggling to see the wood for the trees. (Sorry about the clichés, but they work!) We need to be able to create one image that serves as an advertisement for your book. We should not be inspired to turn your book into an illustrated novel. Focus focus focus.

Objectivity.

Since I ask all my clients to fill in a questionnaire that elicits all the information I need to create a cover that is competitive in the market, I don't need to know everything about your book in order to help your book sell. This helps me focus on what is important: target audience, genre, current market trends, and my own added artistic vision.

Client: I'm sorry, I've found a freelancer more suitable for my needs, but I'd love to hear your thoughts on a couple of the following concepts and what other ideas you might have which could hit that contemporary tone I'm going for...

Me: Er ... no.

I know most of these client conversations have been funny up to this point, but I just want to point out that the previous one isn't. And I know that many people think it's okay to do this. It's really not. It's a bit like walking into a bakery that sells your favorite cake and asking, hey, can I have the recipe for this so that I can make it at home and avoid having to spend money in your shop?

Email correspondence

Please give us time.

Don't be alarmed or disappointed, or annoyed if your designer takes a few days to respond to your emails. If we spent all day answering emails, we'd never get any actual design work done.

There's also the issue of disturbing creative flow. If I'm deep into the design of a project, looking at my emails will jolt me out of my creative headspace. If that happens, it's hard for me to get back in, and I may even lose ideas. I try to respond to emails within seventy-two hours and ninety-five percent of the time I reply within forty-eight hours. Keep in mind, also, that most of us are likely to take weekends off, since this is our day job. I understand, as an author too, that weekends are often used to write and complete writing-related tasks (I'm writing this on a weekend!) since most writers do not have the luxury to quit their day jobs (also me!), so even if you do rattle off a few emails over the weekend, a bit of patience is needed.

Please use clear and relevant subject lines.

Not only does this help me distinguish what's pressing and what's not, but it also helps *you* navigate your correspondence with your designer. I don't know about other designers, but I typically wake up to about twenty to thirty clients emails every morning. It's possible, on one given day, for me to send three different emails to the same client each related to different things. As much as you think it's more efficient to respond to them all in one email, it's actually not, because then it confuses the relationship between the subject line and the content. So, keep your email threads relevant to what's in the subject line. It will make referring to them later a lot easier, if needed.

We are humans with feelings, and limited time, just like you, on the other side of that screen.

With today's texting culture, and the condensed way we interact on social media, it's so easy to rattle off ten separate one-liners as they come to mind. Please don't. Write your thoughts/feedback down on your own notetaking device until you no longer have anything to add. And I suggest you sleep on it! Then when you're able to communicate your thoughts in an organized and concise manner, email your designer. Please also refrain from texting them via Facebook, WhatsApp, Viber, etc. If you want to chat about something, book in a date and time so your designer can be completely present, rather than in the middle of trying to feed their resistant toddler some dinner.

> *Client:* A bit of a time-suck filling in this questionnaire, so I've only filled in half of the details. I'm in Athens right now, so let's meet for a coffee and I can give you all the details about the book cover then.
>
> *Me:* I'm sorry, but if you can't put the work in, then neither can I. I juggle multiple clients every week so I really need all the details in writing.
>
> *Client:* Oops! Sorry, Jessica. I had assumed I was getting your complete and undivided attention for my cover. I hadn't realized a girl needs to work so hard to maintain her standard of living in this Rock 'n' Roll city. Sorry for my presumptuousness.

Phone correspondence

I'm always happy to set up a thirty-minute call, with video on or off, as I'm sure most designers are. But keep in mind that this is just a way for you to get to know us, to put a voice and a face to a name. It will not relieve you of the task of answering the questionnaire or briefing your designer in writing. Since I work with multiple clients at the same time, I need everything in writing so that I can refer to the information when needed. I can't keep everything in my head. But if you have some pressing questions that you'd prefer to talk through rather than type up in an email, a phone call is good for that.

Timeframe

If all goes well, it typically takes me around two weeks to deliver final upload/print-ready cover files from the start date we agree on. When I say "if all goes well," it means that the client has easily chosen a concept from my design samples and has not needed more than the three revisions included in my price. Other designers may work differently, so be sure you acquire this information, and agree on it, before handing over any money or signing any project agreements. It's okay to ask about this information at any time after your initial contact, since the designer may already cover your questions in their first response. I do!

Design inspiration

I send my clients a questionnaire that asks them for lots of information which serves as a brief, but should you be using another designer, you can also use these questions to help guide you in writing up your design brief for them, since they may leave that up to you. A few publishing companies that I work for have actually taken my questionnaire and used it as a base for their own designer briefs, so I know for a fact that it works! Sometimes I don't need *all* this information to design a great cover, but it's very useful to have at hand should I need to refer to it. Here are the questions I include to drum up inspiration:

For fiction

    a. What genre is your book?
    b. What kind of audience are you targeting?

c. What era is your book set in? What aspects of this era are prominent in your book?
d. What is the setting like? Please describe it to the best of your ability. What aspects of this setting are prominent in your story?
e. Describe the appearance of your main characters (eye color, hair color/length/shape, etc.)
f. What are the themes explored in your book?
g. Do you use any recurring symbols (literal or metaphorical) in your book?

For nonfiction

a. What's the subject of focus?
b. Who is your target audience? Please describe the basic profile of your typical reader.
c. What physical objects, environments/settings, if any, are associated with your subject matter? (Stereotypical and unconventional ideas are all helpful.)
d. Are there any key symbols (literal and/or metaphorical) in your book?
e. If applicable, what are the main themes, concepts, and/or messages explored?
f. If applicable, how does the book speak to the reader's desire for emotional growth/enlightenment?
g. If applicable, how will the book change your readers' life, business, or relationships?
h. If applicable, list three to five things your reader will learn.

For my questionnaires in their entirety, refer to Appendix C. I have also included a questionnaire for a logo design, which you may also want to commission for your book covers.

Also, be sure to look at your desired designer's website for packages. You might be able to get a better price if you buy services in bulk. Most designers I know offer packages (I do!) and if they specialize in book covers, they are also likely to offer branding design too, since branding is part and parcel of becoming a published author.

Here's how not to answer my questionnaire:

    a. All Genre's
    b. All Audiences
    c. Current times based upon past history
    d. Spiritual
    e. N/A All
    f. N/A
    g. Answers to Life
    h. No

If you can't describe your own book, how do you expect me to be able to?

How things roll at Jessica Bell Design

Here is an explanation of my process. This is not representative of the way all designers work since I can only speak for myself.

Samples of the front design

When your start date rocks around, I will read through your questionnaire and prepare my brain for another deep dive into a creative realm. If anything is unclear, I'll email you questions. I'll also start looking through stock sites and collecting images that I could possibly use. If I am immediately inspired and hit with ideas, I'll get started on your samples in the same day. If you're super lucky, you may have your three samples the following day. If not, I may need a few days to let ideas percolate before opening Photoshop. The design mind is similar to the writer's mind in that it never stops working, even when we're away from our desks.

Once your three samples are done, I will sleep on them, and see if I want to make any tweaks the next day. You will receive the samples via a link to download them. You will see there are *different* concepts, not three variations of the same concept, which is what I've noticed some other designers do. Typically, Version 1 will be as close to the client's description of what they want as possible, including their own visual ideas (if appealing), but hitting the target audience hard. Version 2 will be my own visual ideas, but still hitting the target audience hard. Version 3 will be a wild card—something that spoke to me artistically that I believe will target your audience in a clever way, but may not be one hundred percent on trend. But that's how new trends get started, isn't it?

So, what happens if you love them all? How do you choose? I have some advice about that.

Firstly, not all designers are happy with their drafts being publicly splashed all over the internet, so before you decide to ask the opinion of your followers, ask your designer for permission.

Once you have their permission solicit votes on social media! It's unlikely that you won't get permission if you ask nicely, and the designer might even give you some useful instruction on how to present them too.

But don't stop there. Use those votes to eliminate *one* design from the samples. Then create a poll on a platform like PickFu. PickFu solicits feedback from readers who don't know you, so that you have real-time objective feedback from a specific audience. If you decide to do this, use my referral link which will give you fifty percent off your first poll: *pickfu.com/jbd*. You pay per poll, and there is no subscription fee, but you will have to sign up for an account.

Lastly, come back to me with the results so that we can discuss them, and I can help you make a decision. Getting outside feedback may also assist both of us in seeing things we should revise.

Revisions

So now you've made a decision on which concept you'd like to move forward with. From this point forward, you have three revisions included in the price. As noted in the section on email correspondence, the best thing for you to do now is to think about any changes, if any, you want to make. Note them down, and email me a digest of your thoughts/required changes. I'll then review your feedback and let you know if there will be any problem implementing anything and why. A possible reason why a specific change might not work is because, technically, it cannot be done. For example, a question I frequently get is, "Can you make the title bigger?" If it's a very long word and it's already touching the margins of the cover, this request is not possible unless I change the font to something with slimmer letters, or bring the letters closer together (called kerning), or completely redesign the cover to something that artistically breaks up the word. Take a look at Figure 99 as an example.

The thing is though, if the cover design looked good with slimmer letters, or reduced kerning, or an artistic unconventional design, I would have done that already. And I also would have tried to make the title as large as possible within the constraints of the existing design. So, if I say no, then please know, I'm not being lazy or stubborn. It's because, aesthetically, it just does not work.

Figure 99

Other file formats

Once the front cover design is finalized, I'll start working on the other cover formats you've asked for. The most typical format that is needed is the paperback cover. This cover will be delivered as one seamless design of the back, spine, and front. I'll send through a Draft 1 of that for you to check over. Changes more than typo fixes aren't generally needed. Once that's finalized and delivered along with any other formats, such as audiobook (front cover rearranged as a square) and hardcover, that's a wrap! You'll receive your upload-ready and print-ready files via a download link. Here's an example of what you'll get:

- 9798985566710_PBcov
- 9798985566727_HBcov
- Ululations_3D-mock-up
- Ululations_AUDcov
- Ululations_eBcov

Key:

String of numbers = ISBN
PBcov = paperback cover
HBcov = hardcover
eBcov = eBook cover
AUDcov = audiobook cover
3D-mock-up = a 3D model of your cover on a book

What a journey!

COST AND RECOMMENDED DESIGNERS

In general, a good cover designer will cost around 500-700 USD for an eBook and paperback cover. Some designers, including myself, also offer packages that include other formats and marketing graphics. So just check your desired designer's website to see what they offer. Don't be shy to ask if they offer something that you can't see on their website! Most websites will not list every possible thing that can be designed, but a designer certainly has the skills to design an album cover, for example, or a movie poster, if they have book cover design experience.

Here is a list of designers, I can personally vouch for:

jessicabelldesign.com (me!)
lawstondesign.com
jdsmith-design.co.uk
metzdesign.com
vanessamendozzidesign.com

Remember to also check out the curated lists in Appendix G.

A Few Last Words (And Connect With Me!)

There is never a last word in book cover design. It's always evolving and changing. The key is to understand your market and audience, and start from there. So instead of closing this book, how about you don't close it. What do you think about flipping back to the beginning of the book and redigesting the book cover designs? Because now, don't you think you'll have a whole new perspective?

For more of my book cover designs, check out *jessicabelldesign.com* and my publishing house website *vineleavespress.com*.

For easy access to all of my covers, including pre-mades, head on over to my *@jessicabelldesign* Instagram profile. If you comment on anything there, please tell me if you have wandered over after reading this book, and I'll follow you right back.

Subscribe to my newsletter: *bit.ly/JBDsignup*

Connect with me on social media:

Instagram: *@jessicabelldesign* and *@yesiamjessicabell*
Twitter: *@iamjessicabell*
Facebook: *@jessicabelldesign* and *@jessbell.vineleaves*
YouTube: *youtube.com/c/msbessiebell*
LinkedIn: *linkedin.com/in/jessicacarmenbell*

Acknowledgements

A huge thanks to Melanie Faith, my development editor, for spotting areas in this manuscript for me to expand upon. She is a genius when it comes to writing reference books, and she helped me fill some very important holes that I didn't realize existed. You should really check out her books for writers (I designed all her covers!) via Vine Leaves Press. Click on *Reference Books for Writers* on our book page here: *vineleavespress.com/books*.

Thank you to Amie McCracken, my Vine Leaves Press partner, who created the InDesign interior template for this book so that I would save time and energy relearning the program after not using it for almost three years! (Pregnancy and motherhood caused that.) Also, for her guidance and support in every single creative thing that I do. I don't know what I would do without her in my life. Oh, and also for brainstorming titles for this book with me. Thank you!

And I mustn't forget, Jean Gill, a client of mine who has hung around for thirty-two book covers (and counting.) I had a bit of a breakdown thinking of ideas for the cover of this book. I put so much pressure on myself. There was no way I was going to get away with a less than super awesome book cover for a book about cover design. I spent a whole day working on a concept that didn't work because I had it in my head that it *should* work. Technically, it worked, but it wasn't *me*. It was just too serious. It needed humor! Jean virtually held my hand through this process and eventually made me realize that I had to step away from it for a while. And it definitely needed a new title. And lo and behold, that same night, when I got talking to Amie, it hit me. If you want to see my rejected cover, ask!

Thank you, also, to all the indie authors who, without hesitation, offered up their DIY book cover designs for potential examples. Your support is incredible! I'm sorry I couldn't include them all in this book.

Appendix A

Jessica Bell Design Attribution License

Date: Month XX, 20XX

Works:

1) Cover design (*Month, 20XX* version) of *Book Title* by Author Name

You are free to:

1) Share — copy and redistribute the material in any medium or format
2) Adapt — remix, transform, and build upon the material for any purpose, even commercially.

The licensor cannot revoke these freedoms as long as you follow the license terms.

License Terms:
1) Attribution — You must give appropriate credit. You may do so in any reasonable manner, but not in any way that suggests the licensor endorses you or your use.
2) The original design remains the intellectual property of Jessica Bell Design.

Appendix B

Jessica Bell Design Project Agreement

This contract is by and between *Publisher Name*, henceforth known as "Publisher," and Jessica Bell, registered under the name of Jessica C. Bell in Athens, Greece, henceforth known as "Designer," for the purposes of coming to terms on the design of four book covers and four logos, henceforth known as the "Project."

This Agreement is set forth on *DATE*.

I. Grant of Rights

The Publisher grants the Designer the right to include, in small print, the following on the imprint page of digital releases, and the back cover of all hard copy formats: *Cover Design by Jessica Bell.*

The Publisher grants the Designer the right to use the completed designs for advertising purposes and to resell any rejected sample designs. The Designer grants the Publisher the right to share and redistribute the completed designs in any medium or format.

If the Publisher would like the ability to adapt — remix, transform, and build upon the material for any purpose, even commercially — a permissions fee of €300 (Three hundred Euros) must be paid. In this case, the complete (or incomplete) layered Photoshop files will be supplied along with an Attributions License. See a sample Attributions License here.

By signing this contract, the Publisher agrees to the Designer's Terms and Conditions as outlined on *jessicabelldesign.com*.

II. The Project

The Designer is obligated to provide the Publisher with the following within the agreed time frame upon receiving a completed Questionnaire accompanied by a 50% deposit (*See Section III. Payment*):

1. 3 x eBook cover design in JPEG
2. 2 x paperback cover in PDF
3. 2 x case laminate in PDF
4. 3 x 3D mock-up in PNG (with transparent background)
5. 4 x logos in various formats
6. An unlimited time to discuss ideas via written correspondence. This includes the Designer providing three mock designs, designed with low-resolution watermarked images for the Publisher to choose from, based on a concept that has been discussed.
7. Up to three image downloads via a stock site. The cost of any extras will be added to the Publisher's bill at 5 Euros per image at the time of project completion.
8. Three rounds of revisions.

III. Payment

Cost: €2400 (Two thousand and four hundred Euros)

The Publisher agrees to pay a 50% deposit to begin the Project, and the outstanding 50% upon completion. Any extra costs incurred during the making of the cover will be added to the second bill.

If the Publisher wishes to terminate the Project before completion, the deposit will not be refunded, nor will the design files in their current state be handed over to the Publisher.

IV. Collaboration

The Publisher agrees to deliver all relevant information in the Questionnaire regarding the Project before the Designer begins work. If the Publisher does not provide the Designer with instructions regarding their vision for the Project, the Designer reserves the right to have creative control. The Publisher retains the right to review the Project during its various design stages, have final approval of the Project's content, and offer any suggestions or bring up any concerns.

Upon the Publisher's approval of the look and feel of the Project, the Designer agrees to provide a maximum of three rounds of revisions. If extra work is needed beyond what is outlined in *Section II. The Project*, the Publisher is required to pay 30 Euros per extra hour spent on the project. The Designer agrees to do the work to the best of her ability to avoid requiring extra time. The only foreseeable reason for this to happen would be if the Publisher is indecisive and/or disagreeable without logical reason.

V. Indemnification

The Designer agrees that she is the sole creator of the Project and has the right to use all images sourced from stock sites for the purpose of the Project. The Publisher indemnifies and holds harmless the Designer against any and all claims, actions, demands, etc. arising from the use of the Project. This includes, but is not limited to, actions involving using copyrighted images that the Publisher may have provided without the artist's consent.

VI. Project Completion

The Designer will provide the final files of the Project no later than the agreed date expressed in writing, unless unforeseeable events occur, through no fault of the Designer, that may delay production. These events include, but are not limited to, crimes against the Designer and labor strikes.

If the Designer fails to provide the Project within one month after the agreed deadline, the Publisher may, at the Publisher's option, by written notice to the Designer, terminate this Agreement and receive a full refund. In such event no damages, suits, actions, or proceedings shall be claimed, instituted or maintained by the Publisher against the Designer.

This Project Agreement is subject to the laws and regulations of Greece. Signed:

_____ _____

Publisher Printed Name   Publisher Signature

_____ _____

Designer Name   Designer Signature

Appendix C: Client Questionnaires

CLIENT QUESTIONNAIRE: FICTION

1. Please insert your cover copy here:

Title:
Author name:
Back cover blurb:
Puff quotes (if available):
Tag line (if wanted on cover):
ISBN:
Price (if you'd like it visible in the barcode):
Publisher/author website URL:

2. Please provide the following cover specifications:

Trim size:
Page count:

For Lightning Source, or IngramSpark (note that if you distribute through either of these platforms you will need your own ISBN):
Paper color (white, crème, or groundwood):
Cover laminate (gloss or matte):

For KDP:
Paper color (white or crème):

Other:
Spine width:
Bleed size:

3. **Please answer the following questions about your book with as much detail as possible:**

    a. What genre is your book?
    b. What kind of audience are you targeting?
    c. What era is your book set in? What aspects of this era are prominent in your book?
    d. What is the setting like? Please describe it to the best of your ability. What aspects of this setting are prominent in your story?
    e. Describe the appearance of your main characters (eye color, hair color/length/shape, etc.)
    f. What are the themes explored in your book?
    g. Do you use any recurring symbols (literal or metaphorical) in your book?

4. **Please copy and paste three to five short excerpts (50-100 words) from your book that are representative of your book as a whole. Please choose excerpts that include vivid imagery.**

5. **Please copy and paste Amazon links to some book covers you love and that are in a similar style to what you want.**

6. **If you have any cover design ideas of your own, please describe them here. But I cannot promise that they will be used.**

CLIENT QUESTIONNAIRE: NONFICTION

1. Please insert your cover copy here:

Title:
Subtitle:
Author name:
Back cover blurb:
Puff quotes (if available):
ISBN:
Price (if you'd like it visible in the barcode):
Publisher/author website URL:

2. Please provide the following cover specifications:

Trim size:
Page count:

For Lightning Source, or IngramSpark (note that if you distribute through either of these platforms you will need your own ISBN):
Paper color (white, crème, or groundwood):
Cover laminate (gloss or matte):

For KDP:
Paper color (white or crème):

Other:
Spine width:
Bleed size:

3. Please answer the following questions about your book with as much detail as possible:

   a. What's the subject of focus?
   b. Who is your target audience? Please describe the basic profile of your typical reader.
   c. What physical objects, environments/settings, if any, are associated with your subject matter? (Stereotypical and unconventional ideas are all helpful.)
   d. Are there any key symbols (literal and/or metaphorical) in your book?
   e. If applicable, what are the main themes, concepts, and/or messages explored?
   f. If applicable, how does the book speak to the reader's desire for emotional growth/enlightenment?
   g. If applicable, how will the book change your readers' life, business, or relationships?
   h. If applicable, list three to five things your reader will learn.

4. Please copy and paste three to five short excerpts (50-100 words) from your book that are representative of your book as a whole.

5. Please copy and paste Amazon links to some book covers you love and that are in a similar style to what you want.

6. If you have any cover design ideas of your own, please describe them here. But I cannot promise that they will be used.

CLIENT QUESTIONNAIRE: LOGO

1. What is the name of your company?
2. Do you have a company tagline or slogan that could be used as part of the logo?
3. What product(s) or service(s) does your business provide?
4. Who is your target audience?
5. Who are your competitors?
6. What differentiates you from your competitors?
7. Why should your audience choose you over the competition?
8. What does your audience care about?
9. How does your audience learn about your product, organization or service?
10. What words do you want your audience to associate with your company?
11. Is there a unique story behind your business?
12. What objects/symbols/visuals do you associate with your business and why?
13. What feeling do you want the logo to convey?
14. Where will your logo be used?
15. Do you want your logo to be an image, text, or a combination of both?
16. What are the first five logos that pop into your head? Do you like/dislike these logos? Why? Why do you think these logos are so memorable?
17. If you already know them, please provide three examples of logos that you like and explain why. (Don't search for any online if you don't know straight off the bat.)
18. If you already know them, please provide three examples of logos that you dislike and explain why. (Don't search for any online if you don't know straight off the bat.)
19. (OPTIONAL) Please provide your own design ideas or expectations, including color and font preferences if you have any:

Appendix D: How to obtain puff quotes

Collecting endorsements (aka puff quotes) for your book is not as hard as you think. Nowadays, you don't need Stephen King to endorse your book in order for it to be credible. Readers don't care. They just want to see that someone else enjoyed the book.

Endorsements can come from other authors or even just other readers. For nonfiction, you can find other professionals in your field or network. You can even submit your book for a free editorial review by a reputable service, such as *Readers' Favorite, Foreword Reviews, BookLife*, or *The Wishing Shelf Award*. I advise against paying for reviews, which I believe is a huge rip-off. There is no evidence anywhere that these things lead to sales. It's all just a big ego boost.

Also, let your endorsement readers know that it is not a requirement to read the entire book, that they can read as much as they like to get a feel for it, or skim it. You understand their time is precious, and it is standard practice for reviewers of this type to not fully read everything they are sent.

Also make sure they provide a by-line, for example:

Jessica Bell, author of GO
or
Jessica Bell, publisher of Vine Leaves Press

Appendix E: How to obtain ISBNs

Here's a list of where you can purchase ISBNs:

Australia
Thorpe-Bowker: *myidentifiers.com.au*
Packages range from a single ISBN to a block of 1,000.

United Kingdom and Republic of Ireland
Nielsen: *nielsenisbnstore.com*
Packages range from a single ISBN to a block of 1,000.

Canada
Library and Archives Canada: *bac-lac.gc.ca*
Free! (The way it should be, in my opinion!)

United States
Bowker: *isbn.org*
Packages range from a single ISBN to a block of 1,000.

The prices vary, significantly. And in many countries, ISBNs are free. Don't ask me why this is the case. I live in Greece and I get mine for free from the National Library of Greece.

If you're not located in any of the above countries, you can obtain ISBNs from your respective national ISBN registration agency.

A directory of ISBN agencies is available here: *isbninternational.org*

Appendix F: Popular trim sizes

4 x 6" (154 x 102mm)
4 x 7" (178 x 102mm)
4.25 x 7" (178 x 108mm)
4.37 x 7" (178 x 111mm)
4.72 x 7.48" (190 x 120mm)
5 x 7" (178 x 127mm)
5 x 8" (203 x 127mm)
5.06 x 7.81" (198 x 129mm)
5.25 x 8" (203 x 133mm)
5.5 x 8.25" (210 x 140mm)
5.5 x 8.5" (216 x 140mm)
5.83 x 8.27" (210 x 148 mm) A5
6 x 9" (229 x 152mm)
6.14 x 9.21" (234 x 156mm)
6.5 x 6.5" (165 x 165 mm)
6.625 x 10.25" (260 x 168mm) (Graphic Novel)
6.69 x 9.61" (244 x 170 mm) (Pinched Crown)
7 x 10" (254 x 178 mm)
7.44 x 9.69" (246 x 189mm)
7.5 x 9.25" (235 x 191mm)
8 x 8" (203 x 203mm)
8 x 10" (254 x 203mm)
8 x 10.88" (276 x 203mm)
8.25 x 10.75" (273 x 210mm)
8.25 x 11" (279 x 210mm)
8.268 x 11.693" (297 x 210mm) A4
8.5 x 8.5" (216 x 216mm)
8.5 x 9" (229 x 216mm)
8.5 x 11" (280 x 216m)

Appendix G: Useful links

References

- Adobe Color Wheel: *color.adobe.com/create/color-wheel*
- PickFu: *PickFu.com* (Use the discount code *jbd* for 50% off first poll)

Printing and distribution partners

- KDP: *kdp.amazon.com*
- IngramSpark: *ingramspark.com*
- PublishDrive: *publishdrive.com*
- Draft to Digital: *draft2digital.com*
- Lightning Source: *lightningsource.com*
- Blurb: *Blurb.com*
- Clays: *clays.co.uk*
- IPG: *ipgbook.com*
- Baker & Taylor: *btpubservices.com*
- Ingram: *ingramcontent.com*

Curated lists and advice

- The Alliance of Independent Authors: *allianceindependentauthors.org* (My affiliate link: *allianceindependentauthors.org/?affid=1327*) and *selfpublishingadvice.org*
- Kindlepreneur: *kindlepreneur.com/book-cover-software-designers-services/*
- The Creative Penn: *thecreativepenn.com/bookcoverdesign*
- John Fox: *thejohnfox.com/2019/09/30-best-book-cover-designers*
- Makeuseof.com: *makeuseof.com/best-ebook-cover-design-services-self-publishing*

Appendix H

JBD BINDING Cheat Sheet

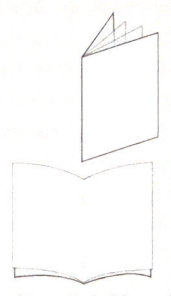

SADDLE STITCHING
8 - 64 PAGES

Sheets of paper (signatures) are nested and stapled together through the center fold with wire staples. Alternatively this can be done with thread which falls into the hand sewn category.

LOOP STITCHING
8 - 64 PAGES

Similar to saddle stitching, sheets of paper (signatures) are stitched together through the spine with loop wire so they can be inserted into a ring binder.

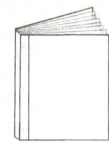

SIDE STITCHING
4 - 160 PAGES

(Stab or Wire Stitched)

Individual sheets are stacked, then stapled together down the side – from the front to the back. Also referred to as stab or wire stitching.

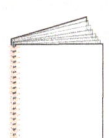

SPIRAL BINDING
4 - 640 PAGES

(Comb, Spiral, Wire)

Individual sheets are fastened together by a continuous spiral of wire or plastic that coils through a series of holes punched along one side of the printed piece.

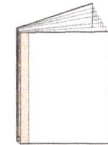

TAPE BOUND
20 - 720 PAGES

Sheets are bound together with an external strip of tape or cloth. To add additional strength, side stitching is often applied.

PERFECT BOUND
40 - 720 PAGES

With the help of a flexible adhesive, folded pages (signatures) are glued together at the spine and a paper cover is wrapped around the whole piece.

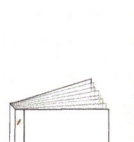

LAY FLAT
80 - 640 PAGES

The same method as perfect binding, but in this case PUR glue, which holds stronger than standard perfect binding glue, is used, as well as stretch paper for the spine. The spine of the book is not attached to the spine of the cover. All in all allowing a publication to lie fully open.

SCREW BOUND
4 - 640+ PAGES

(Chicago Screws, Grommeting, Eyeleting)

Holes are drilled into the pages and cover of a booklet which are then held together by aluminum screw posts. Grommets and eyelets can accommodate up to 120 pages.

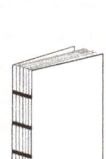

SMYTH BOUND
8 - 720+ PAGES

(Smyth Sewn or Thread Bound)

Folded, gathered and collated pages (signatures) are sewn together at the spine. First through the individual signatures and then, for extra durability and flexibility, these signatures are likewise sewn together with thread. This technique is also referred to as smyth sewn or thread bound.

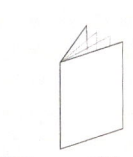
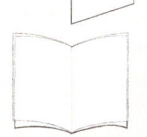

SINGER SEWN
4 - 60 PAGES

(Saddle or Side)

A small number of pages are sewn together through the spine with thread with the help of a converted Singer sewing machine. Singer sewing can be done through the spine or on the side of a brochure (similar to side stitching).

CASE BOUND
24 - 720 PAGES

Case bound books are typically sewn or perfect bound first, then encased with a separately made hard or soft cover.

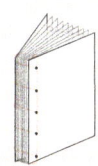

HAND SEWN
4 - 480+ PAGES

(Coptic or Japanese Stab)

Individual sheets are hand sewn together on one side—with needle and thread—in various patterns. As simple as basting or as complex as Japanese stab binding.

Index of Subjects and Images

A

Addey, Melissa, *The Cold Palace* (Edition 1), Figure 7 16
Addey, Melissa, *The Cold Palace* (Edition 2), Figure 8 17
Addey, Melissa, *The Consorts* (Edition 1), Figure 1 10
Addey, Melissa, *The Consorts* (Edition 2), Figure 2 11
Addey, Melissa, *The Forbidden City* series, 2D digital boxed set, Figure 59 68
Addey, Melissa, *The Forbidden City* series, 3D digital boxed set, Figure 58 67
Addey, Melissa, *The Forbidden City* series, paperback cover, Figure 60 69
Addey, Melissa, *The Fragrant Concubine* (Edition 1), Figure 3 12
Addey, Melissa, *The Fragrant Concubine* (Edition 2), Figure 4 13
Addey, Melissa, *The Garden of Perfect Brightness* (Edition 1), Figure 5 14
Addey, Melissa, *The Garden of Perfect Brightness* (Edition 2), Figure 6 15
advanced copies 113
advanced reviews (aka puff quotes, endorsements) 111, 113-114, 164, 166, 169
Ambrose, Lawrence, *Moira the Zorzen War: The Divided Worlds*, Figure 33 46
assistant
    designs of 81, 84
    working with and importance of 80, 87, 90, 142
Atkins, Steven, *Monica's Waltz* (Sample 1), Figure 64 76
Atkins, Steven, *Monica's Waltz* (Sample 2), Figure 65 77
Atkins, Steven, *Monica's Waltz* (Sample 3), Figure 66 77
Atkins, Steven, *Monica's Waltz* (Published Edition), Figure 67 78
attribution license (Jessica Bell Design) 159
Aunos, Marjorie, PhD, *Mom on Wheels: The Power of Purpose for a Parent with Paraplegia*, Figure 41 56
author name 111, 113, 159, 164, 166

B

back cover copy (aka book description, jacket copy) 116-119
Baggott, Helen, *Posted in the Past*, Figure 84 104
barcode 70, 119, 121, 164, 166
Barron, Stephanie, *That Churchill Woman*, Figure 19 35
Battista-Parsons, Elaina, *Italian Bones in the Snow*, Figure 36 50
Bell, Jessica, *Bitter Like Orange Peel* (Edition 1), Figure 42 58
Bell, Jessica, *Bitter Like Orange Peel* (Edition 2), Figure 43 59
Bell, Jessica, *How Icasia Bloom Touched Happiness*, Figure 28 39
Bell, Jessica (cover design and illustration by Janice Phelps Williams), *String Bridge* (Edition 1), Figure 11 29
Bell, Jessica, *String Bridge* (Edition 2), Figure 12. .30
Bell, Jessica, *String Bridge* (Edition 3), Figure 13. .31
Bell, Jessica, *String Bridge* (Edition 4), Figure 14. .32
Biewald, Connie, *Truth Like Oil*, Figure 32. 45
binding cheat sheet. 173
bleed. 122, 164, 166
blurb. 57, 60, 96, 111, 116, 117, 164
Blurb.com. 127, 172
book description (see: back cover copy)
booking a designer 141
boxed set 67-70
Boyce, Niamh, *Inside the Wolf*, Figure 45. 62
branding (for series or collections) 63-72
by-line. 114, 169

C

Caputo, Yvonne, *Dying with Dad*, Figure 39. 54
Clucas, Lauren S, *Choices*, Figure 40 55
clutter (avoid). 40, 44, 47
color (paper options). 125-126
color printing (weight of paper, for children's books, some nonfiction or reference, photography books, graphic novels) 127
color symbolism 47-53
    cover examples 54-45, 58-59, 61-62
    strategy for fiction 60
    strategy for poetry 61-62

strategy for nonfiction 53-59

colored end papers 136

color theory chart, Figure 37 51

common colors chart, Figure 38 52

common trim sizes for novels chart, Figure 89 123

cost

    editorial images 99

    pre-made covers 108

    logo. 121

    barcode and revision of files 121

    trim size 122

    proof copies 129

    leather binding 133

    cost and recommended designers 154

    project agreement. 161

cover finish 128-140, 166

Crawford, Annalisa, *Small Forgotten Moments* (full dust jacket), Figure 88 120

curated lists and advice. 154, 172

D

debossing 130, 133

debossing example, Figure 91 131

Dempsey, Ernest, *The Secret of the Stones*, Figure 18 34

distributor. 96, 121, 122, 129

E

editorial

    images 99

    reviews. 113, 169

email (correspondence tips) 98, 136, 141, 144-146, 149, 151

embossing. 130

embossing example, Figure 91 131

endorsements (aka puff quotes) 113, 117, 169

endpapers (printed or colored) 136

Epstein, Ann S., *The Great Stork Derby*, Figure 52 65

Epstein, Ann S., *On the Shore*, Figure 50 65

Epstein, Ann S., *One Person's Loss*, Figure 53 65

Epstein, Ann S., *Tazia and Gemma*, Figure 51 65

F

file formats 87, 124, 153, 154, 159, 160-162
foil stamping 130, 133
foil stamping example, Figure 92 132
font(s) 5
   amateur/bad design. 63, 73, 77, 151, 168
Francesca, Anna, *The Mystery Passenger on Audoma Air*, Figure 86 112
French flaps (aka French fold and gate fold covers). 133
French flaps example, Figure 94 135
front cover copy 74, 111, 113, 117, 153
Frost, Kate, *The Love Island Bookshop*, Figure 30 42

G

gate fold covers (see: French flaps)
genre. 33, 47, 73, 74, 87, 96, 101, 114, 116, 143, 147, 149, 165
Gidley, Apple, *Have You Eaten Rice Today?*, Figure 70. 83
gilded page edges. 133
gilded page edges example, Figure 93. 134
Gill, Jean, *Arrows Tipped with Honey*, Figure 10 23
Gill, Jean, *Natural Forces Trilogy*, Figure 61 71
Gill, Jean, *Someone To Look Up To* (Edition 1), Figure 76 91
Gill, Jean, *Someone To Look Up To* (Edition 2), Figure 77 91
Gillespie, Tom, *Painting by Numbers* (designer unknown), Figure 80 93
Gillespie, Tom, *The Strange Book of Jacob Boyce*, Figure 81 93
glossy inserts (aka plates) 126, 136
glossy inserts example, Figure 95 137
Goodreads. 57
Gregory, Philippa, *The Other Boleyn Girl*, Figure 20. 35

H

Hackney, Tanya, *Leaving the Safe Harbor,* Figure 34 48
hiring and working with
   a designer 79, 96-97
   a freelance author, editor, or copy writer. 107, 116-117
   an assistant 87-90
Hurwitz, Gregg, *Dark Horse*, Figure 16. 34

I

Image
- space 40-44
- avoid clutter 44-46
- color 47-62
- structure and layout for a series or collections, branding 63-71
- logo 70, 72

imagery (stock) 97-99, 102-103, 149, 161-162
imagery (trim size, bleed) 122-124
importance of (book cover design) 26-39
inspiration 18, 94, 109, 143
- design 147-149, 164-168

ISBN
- importance of 119, 121, 164, 166
- obtaining 170

J

jacket copy, (see: back cover copy)
Jan, Bernard, *Postcards From Beyond Reality*, Figure 35 49
Jessica Bell Design (design process) 149-153
Johnson, Meg, *Without: Body, Name, Country*, Figure 44 61

K

Kelly, Martha Hall, *Lost Roses*, Figure 22 35
kerning 151-152

L

leather binding 133
leather binding example 134
Littlemore, Clare, *Acceptance, The Bellator Chronicles*, Prequel, Figure 54 66
Littlemore, Clare, *Compliance, The Bellator Chronicles*, Book 1, Figure 55 66
Littlemore, Clare, *Defiance, The Bellator Chronicles*, Book 3, Figure 57 66
Littlemore, Clare, *Dependence, The Bellator Chronicles*, Book 2, Figure 56 66
logo 53, 63, 70, 119, 121, 148, 160-161, 168
logo, design examples, Figure 62 72
Lopresti, Aaron (illustration by), Figure 63 75
Luger, James, *Return to Iquitos*, Figure 75 89

M

McGarry, Jackson, *Running on Maybe*, Figure 74 88
metadata. 90
   definition of 129
Morris, Roz (author and design), *Ever Rest*, Owen Gent (illustration), Figure 9 21

N

O

objectivity 143-144
orange covers (internet search image), Figure 85 109

P

page count. 124-125, 164, 166
paper (binding options) 125-129, 173
paper colors 125, 164, 166
paper colors reference, Figure 90 126
Patel, Vaishnavi, *Kaikeyi: A Novel*, Figure 27 36
Patterson, James & Howard Roughan, *Steal*, Figure 15 34
phone correspondence 146
plates (see: glossy inserts)
print-on-demand (aka POD) 125, 127-130, 136
printed or colored endpapers example, Figure 96 138
printing and distribution partners 122, 124, 172
project agreement 160-163
pseudonym 113
puff quotes (see: advanced reviews)

Q

questionnaire(s) 70, 102, 143, 146-149, 161-162, 164-168
   for fiction clients 164-165
   for nonfiction clients 166-167
   for logos 168
Quinn, Kate, *The Alice Network*, Figure 24 35

R

Renwick, Anne, *Kraken and Canals* (Edition 1, author-designed), Figure 82 94
Renwick, Anne, *Kraken and Canals* (Edition 2, Book Fly Design), Figure 83 94
researching (and choosing a designer) 95-100
reviews 38, 57, 113, 128, 169
revision(s) 82, 85, 87, 96-97, 102, 105, 147, 151, 161-162
ribbon marker 136
ribbon marker example, Figure 98 140
Robertson, Michelle, *Hate Mail: Thank You for Reading*, Figure 31. 43
Robotham, Mandy, *A Woman of War*, Figure 23 35
Ryan, L.T., *End Game*, Figure 17 34

S

Shafak, Elif, *The Island of Missing Trees*, Figure 25 36
Shaw, Romer, *Ten Years of Spring* (assistant's design), Figure 68 81
Shaw, Romer, *Ten Years of Spring* (Jessica Bell's revision), Figure 69 82
Silverstone, Dr. Peter, *The Promise of Psychedelics*, Figure 29 41
slip case 133
slip case example, Figure 58, Figure 92 . . . . 67, 132
Soukup, Fredrick, *Blood Up North*, Figure 87 115
space 40-44
spot UV 129, 136
spot UV, example, Figure 97 139
Stevens, GJ, *Capital Action*, Figure 48 64
Stevens, GJ, *The Gemini Assignment*, Figure 49 64
Stevens, GJ, *Lesson Learned*, Figure 47 64
Stevens, GJ, *Operation Dawn Wolf*, Figure 46 64
symbolism (color, basic meanings) 53, 57, 60, 70
    for nonfiction 53-56
    for fiction 57-59
    for poetry 60-62
    business/branding 70
synergy (of text and image) 73-86

T

tag line (definition and example) 114, 164
target audience 74-75, 80, 143, 147-148, 150, 165, 167, 168
text and image synergy. 73-86
Thomas, Paul, *Imago Dei* (assistant's design), Figure 71. 84
Thomas, Paul, *Imago Dei* (Jessica Bell's revision), Figure 72 85
Thomas, Paul, *Imago Dei* (final cover), Figure 73 86
timeframe. 147
trends 19, 33, 37, 109, 143, 150
trim size. . . . . 96, 122-124 , 164, 166
    popular trim sizes. 171

U

unsuccessful
    book cover design defined 27-28
    examples and explication. 28-33

V

Vine Leaves Press 25, 93, 108, 157, 169
vision (artistic) 143

W

Wallace, James, *Sock Puppet*, Figure 99 152
website
    author 96, 98, 119-121
    freelance editorial endorsement. 117, 169
    distributor/printing partner. 124, 127, 136
    designer 148, 154
    Jessica Bell Design 155
    Vine Leaves Press. 155, 164, 166
Williams, Kate, *The Pleasures of Men*, Figure 21. 35

X

Y

Young, Debbie, *Best Murder in Show* (Edition 1), Figure 78. 92
Young, Debbie, *Best Murder in Show* (Edition 2), Figure 79. 92

Z

Zhang, Jenny Tinghui, *Four Treasures of the Sky*, Figure 26. 36

Vine Leaves Press

Enjoyed this book?
Go to *vineleavespress.com* to find more.
Subscribe to our newsletter:

CPSIA information can be obtained
at www.ICGtesting.com
Printed in the USA
BVHW020519261022
650236BV00013B/569